Joe k-lin's

SH

ME

Sandra
ndacht

LIA

Cover Photograph: Marvullo

Cover and Book Design: Geri Wolfe
Page Layout: Anthony Jacobson

Photographs of the Joe Franklin
Collection by Daniel Stone

ISBN 0-87069-435-9

Library of Congress Catalog
Card Number 84-051258

10 9 8 7 6 5 4 3 2 1

Published by

Wallace-Homestead Book Company
580 Waters Edge
Lombard, Illinois 60148

One of the
ABC PUBLISHING
Companies

"There is comfort in knowing about the past. If we make it through such trying times, there is hope that we can make it through whatever the future holds."

— Joe Franklin

In memory of George M. Cohan (Joe's first friend in show business), Eddie Cantor (Joe's idol and friend), and Martin Block (Joe's mentor).

A special thanks to Lois, Joe's wife, for her humor and understanding.

Contents

Introduction

My name is Sandra Andacht. I am an editor, publisher, author, et al., in the antiques and collectibles industry. Because I operate on a limited budget, long ago I became my own agent and public relations person. This requires a number of skills, mixed with lots of *chutzpah* (guts), imagination, and optimism. For years, I envied all the authors who appeared on TV talk shows plugging their books, going from city to city on tour, and being interviewed by reporters from *People* magazine and big-city papers.

Here in New York City, "The Joe Franklin Show" is the best vehicle for publicizing exhibitions, openings of shows on and off Broadway, or newly released books. This long-running show is telecast twice daily over WOR TV (Channel 9 in New York City) and over WOR Cable worldwide. Joe's live radio program, "Memory Lane," is heard every Saturday evening and Sunday morning over WOR radio—not only in the New York City, tri-state area, but as far north as Maine and as far south as Florida.

With a bit of luck, I was able to obtain Joe Franklin's telephone number, so I called his office. Would you believe it? He answered the phone himself. I gave him my name, my occupation, and explained my deep desire to get some much-needed publicity for my new book. I was amazed when he said that he knew who I was. In fact, he was an avid reader of one of my feature columns. He gave me a date and time for taping and spoke with me for a few minutes. When he found out that this was to be my first TV appearance, he assured me that losing my TV "virginity" would be an enjoyable experience.

Traveling on the Long Island Expressway, especially during rush hour, is an extraordinary challenge. But since I'd left early, I arrived at the studio an hour ahead of schedule. I was shown to a waiting area filled with guests, celebrities, and agents. Why all of them were so nervous escaped me. I knew this would be a one-shot deal, lasting maybe five minutes, and it seemed senseless to become nervous. Joe came over and introduced me to his other guests, including the two who would appear with me—Jake LaMotta (the real Raging Bull) and Tiny Tim.

Joe with the real "raging bull," Jake LaMotta.

I was asked to sit in the seat next to Joe. This, you understand, is equivalent to having lunch with the president or the queen of England. Not many guests are extended such a courtesy on their first appearance unless they are celebrities.

When the red camera light blinked on, Joe held up my book and asked me to introduce myself to his audience. I spoke until the first break. At that point, I thanked Joe for his generosity and was about to get up and leave when he asked me to stay and chat with his other guests. Anyone else might have been rendered speechless. But by this time, Joe knew that he wouldn't have to worry about that problem with me. I spoke with his guests and shared their interests as well as my own. The experience was splendiferous. But when the tapings were done, I was even more thrilled when Joe invited me to his inner sanctum—his office.

Joe's office overlooks Times Square (Broadway and Forty-Second Street). The office is crammed from floor to ceiling and wall to wall with thousands of records and LPs, reels of film, cabinets overflowing with sheet music and lobby cards, personal mementos, signed photographs, and special tributes to and from Joe. Flowing in and out was a steady stream of people—celebrities, agents, messengers, stars yet to be discovered. The phones were always ringing or busy. I couldn't imagine why he wanted me there.

Joe handed me a cup of coffee and a doughnut and asked me to relax and enjoy. He said, "Sandra, we have a great deal in common. We share a love for collecting—for the old, the offbeat, the rare, the unique. I think we'll get along tremendously well."

Then he took me by the hand, leaving an office full of people, escorted me to one of his storage vaults, and allowed me to glimpse a unique side of his personality that the public knows little about—his extraordinary affection for show business memorabilia. Realizing I was overwhelmed, Joe said, "You ain't seen nothin' yet!" He was right. What I saw that day was merely a sneak preview of coming attractions. It still seems inconceivable that one person could have gathered so many mementos.

Joe invited me to make another appearance on his show. "Sandra," he said, "I need a resident antiques expert—someone who will come on from time to time, talk about collecting, and share insights with my guests. You could talk about whatever you think my audience would find interesting." Of course, I accepted.

From this meeting, our friendship and mutual interests grew. And so did my curiosity about Joe and his collection. I learned that Joe is the editor of *Joe Franklin's Memory Lane News,* a bimonthly publication for collectors, dealers, and investors. And I found that his vast collection (the largest amassed by any known individual) covers the world of entertainment and show business from 1900 on.

Joe's collection reflects the evolution of our society through theatre, song, radio, movies, early TV, and all other facets of the entertainment industry. It is an historical record, covering two world wars, the Great Depression, changes in technology, fashion, art, politics, humor, and much more. It allows us to examine changes in life styles over a span of more than fifty years.

Joe's office, with Ben Turpin in the background.

Joe at a party with Martin Mull.

I started writing articles about Joe and the memorabilia he had gathered. But I soon realized that the subject was too overwhelming for articles. I needed to write something more encompassing—something that would reveal Joe's insights into show business, relate some of his experiences, and, of course, properly describe his collection. The vehicle I needed was a book. When I mentioned the idea to Joe, he responded, "Sandra, you're the boss!"

Joe Franklin deserves our accolades for single-handedly preserving an important part of this country's heritage. The following pages were written with love and affection for a man and his collection.

1
The Days of Records and Radio

I am a part of all that I have met;
Yet all experience is an arch where through
Gleams that unhoveled world, whose margin fades
Forever and forever when I move.
—Tennyson

In more than thirty-five years as host of his own television talk show, Joe Franklin has interviewed more than 75,000 guests. They've discussed basketball, yoga, weaving, Italian cooking, and child psychology. And Joe Franklin has absorbed it all, asking numerous questions that make him, in his words, "the oldest permanent student in the world." But long before television took over home entertainment, Joe's interest in show business began thanks to records and radio.

In 1937, at the age of nine, Joe's mother took him to a Broadway show called *I'd Rather Be Right* (short for "I'd Rather Be Right Than President"). The star of that show was George M. Cohan, the established actor and composer of such well-known songs as "Yankee Doodle Dandy" and "You're a Grand Old Flag."

In 1940, Joe ran into Cohan in Central Park. By this time, Cohan's fame had faded, and he was flattered that young Joe recognized him. "I'm Joe Franklin," he said, "and I write for my school newspaper. I'd love to interview you." Not only did Joe get the interview, he got an invitation to Cohan's house for dinner.

The typical teenager, Joe asked if Cohan had ever made a phonograph record. In response, Cohan pulled a one-sided Victor 78 record from a closet. Recorded in about 1911, it was a ten-inch shellac record. According to the purple label, it was titled, "You Won't Do Any Business If You Haven't Got a Band." Cohan autographed it for Joe, "To a good kid—Joe Franklin."

When Joe took the record home and played it, he "became fascinated by the sound, the flavor, the rhythm, the bounce of the vaudeville style. The lyrics were and still are marvelous!" With that enthusiasm, Joe decided to collect all seven of the records Cohan had made. His search was the beginning of his interest in show biz memorabilia.

10

A priceless photo-graph of Joe Franklin as he appeared at age seventeen, doing his first radio show titled "Vaudeville Isn't Dead."

George M. Cohan, 1932, $20-25.

"I made the rounds of antiques shops, junk stores, and the like. I looked through old telephone directories at the library, looking for stores that might still be in business. I figured if these stores had basements for storage, I might be able to go rummaging through them and I could possibly find the old records.

"My enterprise and innovation enabled me to find a few of the seven records I was searching for. And I found other old records that turned me on too—records by Eddie Cantor, Al Jolson, Sophie Tucker, Harry Richman, Georgie Jessel, Bob Hope, Bing Crosby, Morton Downy, and some non-vaudevillians.

"I figured that, if Cohan had made seven records, maybe Eddie Cantor, Rudy Vallee, Kate Smith, and Al Jolson had each made ten. I found out, to my surprise, that they had made thousands and thousands of records. Back in the old days, the home phonograph (hand-cranked, wind-up Victrola) was just about the main source of home entertainment.

"One could say that, inadvertently, I found my life's work cut out for me. And that was to try to secure every record ever made during the entire period of vaudeville." Today Joe owns 75,000 to 100,000 rare 78s in mint condition. According to Joe's specifications, the shellac "must be so shiny, so crisp, that you could shave in it."

The collection began to grow during the summer of 1946, when Joe worked as the record selector for disc jockey Martin Block at WNEW in New York City. Joe studied Block's phrasing and technique as he helped with the show "Make-Believe Ballroom." And his enthusiasm paid off. "One day," Joe says, "Martin asked if I'd like to have my own radio show. Naturally I said I'd love it. He was half kidding, half serious. But he said, 'Look, Joe, I'll get you your own show, fifteen minutes nightly, here at WNEW. But you gotta promise not to compete with me. You gotta play the old stuff you always talk about.'"

Harry Richman, 1932,
$10-15.

Al Jolson, 1939, **$25-35.**

Sophie Tucker in the role of Mother Ralph, guardian angel of Ronald Sinclair, Mickey Rooney, and Judy Garland in M-G-M's Thoroughbreds Don't Cry, *1937,* **$10-15.**

Thus, at the age of eighteen, Joe began his own radio program, called "Vaudeville Isn't Dead." On the first broadcast, Joe introduced records by describing them as "a collector's item worth five hundred dollars" (or some other made-up figure). To his surprise, the impact of his show was immediate.

"The day after my first broadcast, I went back to the junk shop where I was buying my old records off the dusty shelves at the back of the store. And I gave the proprietor the dime or nickel I usually paid. The owner said,

Joe with Eddie Cantor, 1954.

'Why are you giving me a dime? A guy on the radio last night said these records are worth five hundred dollars.' That's how I accidentally created the rare record market."

Within a few months, old records had been featured in *Billboard, Metronome, Cash Box,* and other publications. Joe was gaining quite a reputation, too, as "the young wreck with the old records."

Today, old records are still Joe's first love in collectibles. But as Joe expanded his career, his interest in memorabilia grew, too.

Joe in one of his first offices. Notice the collectibility of the advertisement for "ZUD," an early sponsor. Candid photos are difficult to find. If in mint condition, they become quite valuable.

Amos 'n' Andy (Freeman Gosden and Charles Correll), 1951, $75-100.

Joe's radio remembrances

Amos 'n' Andy. According to Joe, the popularity of this classic radio program was so complete that listeners all across the country interrupted their evenings to catch the latest episode. "Movie theaters," remembers Joe, "interrupted their films and wheeled radios on stage to play the evening adventure for their audiences. Even telephone switchboards would become silent.

"At first, the show aired at eleven o'clock in the East so it could be heard live. That meant it was heard live at ten, nine, and eight o'clock in various parts of the country. Parents in the East found the late hour difficult because their children wouldn't go to bed until the show was over. So NBC switched the time to seven o'clock. More than 100,000 letters of protest poured in from across the country. The problem was solved when NBC staged two separate broadcasts, four hours apart."

Don Carney. This famous radio personality was Uncle Don to millions of kids during the Depression. With the beginning of his theme song, "Hello, nephews, nieces mine, I'm glad to see you look so fine," millions of children across the country tuned in. One of the features of his show was an annual talent contest for his listeners. Uncle Don sent the winning children to Hollywood to make a screen test with the likes of Ethel Barrymore, Fibber McGee and Molly, or Jane Withers.

*Uncle Don, auto-
graphed, $75-100.*

According to Joe, Uncle Don was the victim of an errant story that ruined his reputation. "There was a story that went around," Joe explains, "that one night Uncle Don thought his program was finished and said goodnight the way he always did. According to the story, Uncle Don mistakenly thought the microphone was disconnected and said, 'Well, I hope that will hold the little bastards until tomorrow.' But that never really happened. It was a figment of the imagination of a columnist in Boston who had nothing to write one day and made it up.

"The story spread like wildfire and hurt the career of Uncle Don Carney very much. He was the victim of the kind of narrowmindedness that destroys. Uncle Don was branded a fraud and died of a broken heart. I didn't matter to those who used a fraudulent story that they had perpetrated a bad joke with grave consequences.

"Now he's gone, but certainly not forgotten, because no night was ever complete if you couldn't listen to the friendly, warm, and wonderful voice and manner of Uncle Don Carney."

Guess who said it. "Guess who said the following," says Joe, "and you'll win the $64 question.

"'What could we do without a radio? At any hour of the day or night, tune in and somebody is telling you how to live, how to vote, how to drink, how to think, when to wash your teeth, when to wash your hair, when to cut your whiskers, when to see your doctor, and how to see your doctor, and when to see your priest, and when to see your preacher, and how to put on fat, and how to take it off, and how to make the skin stay white, and how to make it stay black.

"'Honest, no other nation in the world would stand for such advice as that. But we do, and we like it. So the only thing that can make us give up our radio is poverty. The old radio is the last thing to go out of the house when the sheriff comes in.

"'It's an invention that has knocked nobody out of work and that gives work to many people. That's something you can't say for many inventions. So, as bad as it is, I don't know, it's the best invention I think that has ever been.'

"Who said it? Will Rogers, something of a prophet. Here we are in the 1980s, approaching a new century, and we are still affixed to the radio."

Will Rogers, 1921,
$20-30.

An Uncle Don bank (one of Joe's favorite pieces), **$25-30.**

Don Ameche strolling down Memory Lane with Joe.

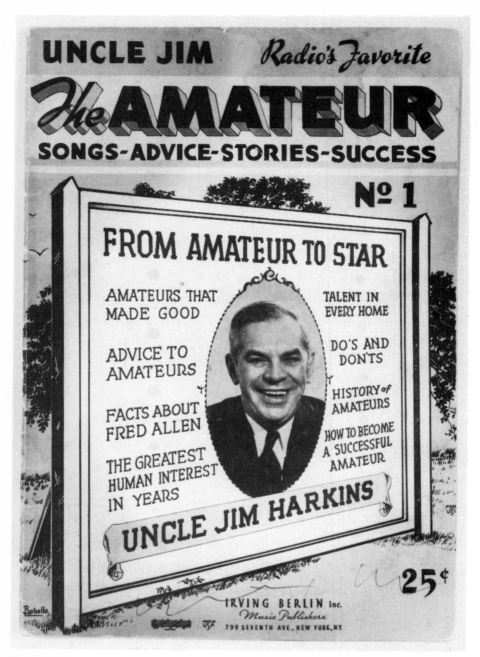

The Amateur, *1935,* **$8-10.**

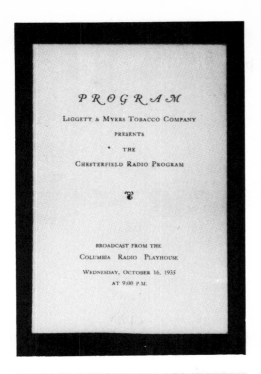

*The Chesterfield Radio Program,
October 16, 1935, featuring Lily
Pons and Andre Kostelanitz, con-
ductor,* **$10-15.**

Radio Program Weekly, *June 30,
1927, containing articles, advice to
the lovelorn, and a weekly radio
schedule,* **$35-45.**

ROTH PARK
NEWS OF THE WEEK

Vol. 4   PROGRAM WEEK OF JANUARY 1   No. 2

THE CRITICS THUNDERED LAVISH PRAISE FOR

"RAINBOW ON THE RIVER"

— AND —

"WINTERSET"

AND IT IS INDEED A PLEASURE TO PRESENT
TO YOU BOTH THESE FINE PRODUCTIONS !

———

BOBBY BREEN

EDDIE CANTOR'S LITTLE WONDER BOY

WILL MAKE YOUR HEART RING IN THIS YEAR'S
SURPRISE MUSICAL
"RAINBOW ON THE RIVER"

———

"WINTERSET"

Acclaimed as the Best Play of the Year is Our Choice
for the Greatest Picture of a DOZEN Years !

Weekly program, featuring Bobby Breen, one of Eddie Cantor's protégés,
$5-6.

Robert Taylor, the M-G-M Radio Movie Club, June 24, 1936, **$10-15.**

Tickets from two radio shows. Krueger Musical Toast, October 15, 1935, featured Ray Block's orchestra. The second ticket is for Duffy's Tavern, 1941. The value of each ticket is **$30-40.** Radio memorabilia is becoming more expensive and difficult to obtain.

*Dan Dailey as
Joe's guest.*

Joe with Jackie Cooper.

TOWN HALL TONIGHT

"An Hour of Smiles"

I P A N A   A N D   S A L   H E P A T I C A

Featuring

FRED ALLEN, THE IPANA TROUBADOURS
and THE SAL HEPATICA SINGERS

with

"2"   Lennie Hayton, the Town Hall Quartet, Portland Hoffa, Jack Smart, Minerva Pious, Eileen Douglas, and John Brown   "2"

Tonight Fred Allen again leads the parade into Town Hall for another hour of laughter. He rides a chestnut charger borrowed from the milk man. And that's the only chestnut allowed tonight. While the amateurs wait, he'll make monkey business of the weekly events. More fun than a barrel of Tarzans. Then Portland unearths the poet, Mr. Bowers, whose doggerel has its day. Next you'll hear the Mighty Allen Art Players in a mystery melodrama entitled "Where are Your Rubbers Darling?—There's Dirty Work Afoot." Then the amateurs crowd in for your cheers of both varieties. And finally the lucky winners will be announced.

Program

1. SMILES—The Ipana Troubadours
   The straight and narrow path leads to Town Hall. Mr. Allen is wreathed in smiles and a Tuxedo.

2. CA C'EST PARIS—The Ipana Troubadours
   Any of the amateurs who feel themselves weakening, can go home to mother at this time.

3. GOT ME DOIN' THINGS—The Sal Hepatica Singers and the Ipana Troubadours
   Presenting that shrewd surveyor of the civic scene . . . that encyclopaedic well of knowledge drilled and ready to gush . . . Fred Allen, who brings you this Town Hall News. Chicago food prices soar. Butchers expect to make more out of three little pigs than Walt Disney did . . . Fritz Kreisler discovered as author of "Turkey in the Straw" . . . Theatrical critic refuses to review work of actors picketing in waiters' strike . . .

4. I BELIEVE IN MIRACLES—The Ipana Troubadours with Lennie Hayton at the piano
   Now for Portland and her receding poet. For half a dollar, he'll find a rhyme for vacuum cleaner.

5. PUSH CART PETE—The Sal Hepatica Singers and the Ipana Troubadours

After this number comes an announcement regarding a subject of importance to all of us—health (adv.).

6. THE MIGHTY ALLEN ART PLAYERS
   Mr. Allen playing the mighty lead in another Charlie Chin Mystery melodrama, "Confucius say man who can cure himself is no ham."

7. RHYTHM MAKES THE WORLD GO ROUND—The Sal Hepatica Singers and the Ipana Troubadours
   During this number the amateurs are clearing their throats and someone else is polishing the gong.

8. THE AMATEURS
   They're here from far and near. First prize is $50 and a week's engagement at the Roxy Theatre. Second, $25.

9. JUST ONCE TOO OFTEN—The Ipana Troubadours
   Mr. Allen will now read the applause machine and the fortunes of the youngsters.

10. SMILES—The Ipana Troubadours
    Our theme song again. May it remind you of a pleasant evening and a couple of fine products.

This is an hour of smiles. Of smiles that come from teeth made gleaming white with Ipana. Of smiles that come from a sense of well-being provided by Sal Hepatica. During the show you will learn how surely and quickly Sal Hepatica relieves troubles due to faulty elimination . . . those dull headaches, listlessness, that "tired feeling" and digestive disorders. Try Sal Hepatica, the *mineral salt* laxative that acts gently—thoroughly—safely. It has been prescribed by doctors for more than forty years. You can get it at any drug store. Try Ipana, too. Ipana and massage is the perfect way to keep your gums healthy, your teeth bright, between regular visits to your dentist. Get a tube of Ipana at your druggist's on your way home. And smile.

February 13, 1935 — 9 P. M., E. S. T., WEAF and Associated Stations

Program for Town Hall Tonight, sponsored by Ipana and Sal Hepatica, February 13, 1935. This show featured Fred Allen. **$7-10.**

Radio Guide, *June 6, 1936,* **$40-50.**

Stars of Radio. *The cover features Jack Benny, Kate Smith, Uncle Ezra, and Gracie Allen.* **$35-40.**

2
An Evening with Joe

On Saturday evening from 7 to 9:30, and again from midnight to 5 a.m., millions of listeners from Maine to Florida are glued to their radio, much as Depression families were in the pre-TV era. Nostalgiacs—people who love the good sounds—enjoy hours filled with memories, both old and new. They hear old radio broadcasts and early LPs, and they listen as Broadway shows come alive again, all thanks to Joe Franklin and his guests.

Joe's listeners range in age from teenagers to septuagenarians. Joe is featured on MTV because of the tremendous interest in his kind of nostalgia by the younger generation, and he just made his first video. There is no one more qualified than Joe Franklin to inform and enrich newcomers and long-time connoisseurs of American entertainment. And he does it with his golden voice, perfect diction, and special way of phrasing that makes him always imitated, but never duplicated. Let's "listen" to excerpts from "An Evening with Joe."

"Welcome to WOR radio, 710 AM, the heart of New York! Our warmest memories somehow do reappear. Bringing back all the scenery, bringing back all the romance of years gone by. This is Joe Franklin saying a good, good evening.

(We hear the haunting melody of Joe's theme song, "Memory Lane.")

"Joe Franklin, again saying good evening. The best of the weekend is yet to come, because we're doing our thing—memory laning together. This is the night of many lilting surprises.

"Our quarter hour (the opening segment), always surefire, anxiously awaited by many of our young oldtimers, is called Frank Sinatra Time. From many decades ago, Frankie Boy with Harry James, singing 'Castle Rock.'. . . .

"Joe Franklin, hosting a program I might subtitle, 'I Remember It Well'— memories that do not fade away. We're doing songs, my friends, as they were sung.

"It's a pleasure to say happy birthday to Rudy Vallee, who is now eighty-three years young! And in a little while, it'll be recollections of Rudy when he was about twenty-eight and radio's number one singing idol. His hit songs

Frank Sinatra, "The Voice," 1942. Joe also calls Frank, when remembering the early days, "Young Blue Eyes." **$50-75.**

Rudy Vallee, 1942, **$10-15.**

were many. Rudy will be honored tonight in our little program-within-the-program featuring Rudy Vallee when he was really and truly the Michael Jackson and Elvis Presley of early-day network radio.

"Every Thursday night from 8 to 9 p.m., from 1928 to 1929, Rudy Vallee's variety show (presented by, I believe, Fleischmann's Yeast) was without question the highest rated radio show. Ladies—especially the young ladies—cried out. They were screaming and screeching for Rudy Vallee back in those days, long before the days of Young Blue Eyes. We are still in our quarter hour, devoted to Young Blue Eyes every Saturday night.

"I thought it might be fun to recall Saturday night about forty years ago. The program that was most popular was called 'Your Hit Parade."

"That radio show had many famous vocalists—Andy Russell, Barry Wood, Dick Todd, Lannie Ross. But the one and only, the one who made big-time history, was a young man named Frank Sinatra. Frank Sinatra, Young Blue Eyes, on 'Your Hit Parade.' "

(From "Your Hit Parade," Joe's audience hears a drum roll and "Number one. Yes, friends, this is the song that's top this week. The song the survey finds at the very head of Your Hit Parade. Frank Sinatra sings the number one song on Your Hit Parade . . ." There are the screams of young bobbysoxers, then the voice of Frank Sinatra singing, "I'll Walk Alone." The audience screams throughout the song, and Sinatra's song ends to fervent applause and more screaming.)

"I wish I could have been in that audience applauding that night. 'Your Hit Parade,' those memorable radio years with Mark Warnow and His Orchestra and a young vocalist named Frank Sinatra, a recent graduate of Tommy Dorsey's orchestra. And this is *your* Memory Lane parade . . .

"Later on tonight, we'll hear some more of those great Hit Parade vocalists from the original tracks. There were so many. We're going to do a few of them. I know that they included Barry Wood, Joan Edwards, Laurence Tibbit, Doris Day, of course, Frankie Boy (The Voice—Young Blue Eyes), Bea Wayne, Buddy Clark, Ginnie Simms, Dorothy Collins, Lannie Ross, Andy Russell, and Snookie Lanson.

"This is your Memory Lane parade, your cavalcade of way back then. I'm very happy to be with you and you and you. Proud to be part of your weekend over the star of New York—WOR. We're loaded down with surprises, presents, and gifts—many precious gifts, elegant ones, beautiful ones. Namely, the stars and the songs of bygone days, in their heydays, when the stars and the songs that they sang were being hailed by people like Walter Winchell. Walter Winchell would have said, 'Tops in town!' Or maybe he would have said, 'An orchid to . . .' That was his phrase.

"This part of our show could be subtitled 'Forever Frank.' A lot of mail for a young Frankie Boy's rendition of 'Stormy Weather.' And here's Frank—Young Blue Eyes— with *Pocketful of Miracles*. In that movie, Bette Davis portrayed Apple Annie, a Daymon Runyan person. Just from memory, I seem to recall Thomas Mitchell, Hope Lange, Glenn Ford, and Peter Falk in *Pocketful of Miracles*.

"We're reviewing the long and honorable recording career of a young man named Frank Sinatra. And here's Frank with 'Oh What It Seemed to Be.'

■

Lannie Ross, "Your Hit Parade," 1933, **$5-10.**

Frank Sinatra, 1953, **$40-50.**

Bing Crosby and Frank Sinatra in a scene from High Society. *The movie also starred the late Princess Grace of Monaco, Grace Kelly.* **$10-15.**

"Joe Franklin, memory laning, and don't forget that week after week, year after year, we've been involved in a longstanding custom that is known as memory laning. And now, how about Young Blue Eyes and 'Call Me Irresponsible.'

■

"Joe Franklin, presenting The Voice every Saturday night. The Voice—another name for Young Blue Eyes, the man with the magic.

"And now, as advertised and by popular demand, our little birthday salute for the man with the megaphone, eighty-three years young, the first crooner—the vagabond lover when he was the number one singing idol—Rudy Vallee, unbelievably popular when he sang 'Betty Coed' and 'The Maine Stein Song.'

■

"We're hearing songs, my friends, as they were sung in the refreshing fashion, the most debonair fashion of the young man—and I do mean young—named Rudy Vallee. Would you believe there was a very elegant cabaret, a most sophisticated nightspot years ago called the Villa Vallee, where you could actually see and hear Rudy Vallee and his Connecticut Yankees in person? But, as is the case nowadays with Michael Jackson, you couldn't get near the place unless you knew the boss. It was always SRO—standing room only—for Rudy Vallee.

"I'm with you wandering through Memory Lane, living the years of laughter and tears. I would say mostly laughter. I'd like to say this is Memory Lane, where all the memories are happy ones. This is your party. Don't forget we are now doing two parties. We are, as the old show business cliché goes, 'by popular request,' doing two Memory Lane programs these weekends. Two beautiful voyages back to our childhood days—the days of the big bands,

George Burns and Gracie Allen, 1939, $30-40.

the comedians, the crooners, the singers, jitterbugging, riding in the rumble seat, or maybe cruising down Fifth Avenue here in New York City in that old, open, double-decker bus. But the program is known as your past—your perfect past, I hope—to see and feel and hear and enjoy the best of way back then and re-experience it to the fullest.

"And certainly the best was Rudy Vallee on the radio. His opening theme song was called 'My Time Is Your Time,' and his closing theme song was 'I'm Just a Vagabond Lover.'

■

"Joe Franklin, hoping you're feeling 100 percent great. Everything is coming up roses as we do our beautiful memories over WOR, 710 AM, the star of New York, honoring the eighty-third birthday of Rudy Vallee, that romantic vagabond lover crooning his songs through a megaphone and winning those jazz-worn audiences very easily with something they needed. Something known as a very relaxed and appealing style. As they say nowadays, he was so 'laid back.' When everyone else was yelling and screaming, he was soft and purring and intimate. Today, of course, the microphone has replaced the megaphone.

"By the way, speaking of microphones, we should at least mention the fact that Rudy Vallee gave the first radio exposure ever to Eddie Cantor, Burns and Allen, Joe Penner, Bob Hope, Alice Faye, Victor Borge, Edgar Bergen with Charlie McCarthy and Mortimer Snerd, and dozens of other stars who got their own radio shows after appearances on the Rudy Vallee program. I must mention that Rudy's number of hits was staggering. Let me just do one, one of the many, many multimillion sellers. How about 'Vini Vini.'

■   33

Edgar Bergen and
Charlie McCarthy.

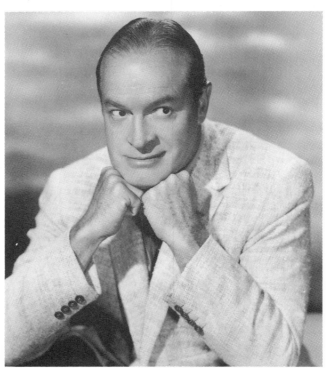

Bob Hope, 1953, **$10-15.**

34

"Always charming, a superstar before that term was invented. Rudy Vallee, happy eighty-three years young! Joe Franklin, your host, with the most memorabilia. I'm strolling with your through Memory Lane. We'll break for news and then we'll be back till 9:30, and then back at 12:05 for the midnight marathon.

"Honestly, I am very happy to be memory laning with you. Here's a lady who honestly deserves to be remembered. Gone but not forgotten. One of the greats—Miss Billie Holiday singing "I Get Along Without You Very Well. . . ."

■

"What a collector's item! What a voice! That's a satiny voice. That's a lady in satin. I would say Billie Holiday was a special artist, a very special lady, a lady of talent and grace. She was called 'Lady Day.' Once upon a time she wrote a best-selling autobiography called *Lady Sings the Blues,* which became a movie later on with Diana Ross. I would imagine that few singers have suffered so much and paid such penalties for a career and had so few pleasant memories of fame as did the late Billie Holiday. And because we know her so well through her book, we find a more personal meaning in her songs. It's so easy to believe what she sang. Her name was Billie Holiday, and she'll sing again.

"Joe Franklin, doing Memory Lane—a little street where old friends meet—an old-fashioned way. Billie Holiday back in the days when she was slender, pretty, and in her glamorous new wardrobe. We find it hard to believe that trouble tagged her for so long, but it did. Billie Holiday as she recorded "For All We Know'. . . .

■

"She was a great and striking singer, the late Billie Holiday. I know what you're wondering, what you're asking. I can feel your vibrations through the microphone, through these airwaves. You're asking, 'Joe, are you gonna play Billie Holiday on the late show?' The answer is absolutely yes! We must do Billie Holiday on the midnight program.

"And now some memories of old Broadway with Ray Bolger playing the title role in *Where's Charlie.*

(Ray Bolger sings, "Once in Love with Amy.")

"That was a song indelibly associated with Ray Bolger, and justly so because nobody could sing that lilting song with the charm and affection of that very talented Ray Bolger.

"People are calling in, asking if that was the same Ray Bolger who portrayed the scarecrow with Judy Garland in a certain little movie called *The Wizard of Oz.* Ray Bolger was the scarecrow; Jack Haley, the late, great Jack Haley, portrayed the Tin Man (not the Thin Man, but the Tin Man); and Bert

Ray Bolger, 1942,
$10-15.

Ray Bolger, 1942,
$10-15.

Jack Haley (The Tin Man), Judy Garland (Dorothy), and Ray Bolger (The Scarecrow), 1939, **$15-20.**

Jimmy Durante and Buster Keaton, 1932, **$35-45.**

Lahr played the Cowardly Lion. The *Wizard of Oz,* of course, was Frank Morgan. And please, my friends, never forget Billie Burke and Margaret Hamilton. They must be mentioned. People doing quiz shows or playing trivia ask about the Thin Man, and then they say the Thin Man was William Powell. The Thin Man was a man named Edward Ellis.

"This is Joe Franklin sharing nostalgia, sentimentalia, memorabilia on Memory Lane. Now, memories of the old Ed Sullivan Show with the Kirby Stone Four with 'Baubles, Bangles, and Beads.'

■

"That came from a Broadway show and movie called *Kismet.* This is Joe Franklin remembering the Kirby Stone Four. I knew Kirby Stone. He's no longer with us, but the memories do remain.

Dean Martin, 1958,
$10-15.

Joe with Jerry Lewis.

"Joe Franklin doing all the memories on Memory Lane. The mailing address is J. F., WOR Radio, New York, New York 10018. We deal in friends, we deal in friendships, old and new. Joe Franklin once again saying good, good evening and, as always, I promise you a very special radio treat.

"A few minutes, right now, with a great star. All I've got to say is 'Jimmy Durante.' What do you say except that he was the greatest. He will not be forgotten. The man that sang 'Inka Dinka Do.' In this particular case, tonight, 'Goodnight, Mrs. Calabash' preceded by 'I Like People.' Jimmy Durante! And this is Joe Franklin, who says I like memories—memories that do not fade away over 710, the star of New York, WOR.

■

"Ladies and gentlemen, tall-dark-handsome Mr. Nonchalant, back in the days when he was the vital half of one of the greatest comedy teams in entertainment history. His name is Dean Martin. The comedy team with those hilarious antics was Dean Martin and Jerry Lewis. We give you a young man, Dean Martin, way down Memory Lane. Dean Martin, and I do mean youngster, as he recorded 'Come Back to Sorrento.'

■

"There's a very tender performance. There is a full, rich baritone. The voice of Dean Martin, who'll do one more tender ballad called 'Just One More Chance,' as soon as I say I'm with you wandering through Memory Lane over the one and only WOR 710 AM.

"'Please take me back for just one more chance.' And that's a good subtitle for our radio program—for our radio party. Please take me back, back to the good old days of once upon a time. Joe Franklin doing happy memories.

"That was Dean Martin singing a Bing Crosby song. Later on we'll have Bing Crosby in 1931. That was Bing's first *big* year, 1931.

"The mail has been pouring in for the crooners. We gave you Frank. We gave you Rudy. We gave you Dean. And now, over WOR in New York City, an RKO radio station, I give you Jerry Vale, whose hair nowadays is so silvery gray. Back in the days when his hair was jet black, he was doing 78 after 78 RPM hit, including 'Pretend You Don't See Her,' and then an encore.

■

"And there's the young man you've been requesting. We gave you a pair of hits of yesteryear by a young fellow who sings those romantic ballads. He sings those love songs in a big voice, without tricks, without any gimmicks, and with great emotional appeal. His name is Jerry Vale.

"This is Joe Franklin saying once again, good evening to you and you and you and welcome to the big party. This is your Memory Lane party. And now, my friends, we present by popular demand another one of our programs

*Mike Nichols and
Elaine May, 1960,
$10-15.*

*"Joe Franklin is the greatest and a joy to know. When Joe plays my
records on Saturday nights, there's always a little something extra that he
says that gives them more importance. He's a fine gentleman and a dear
friend and I love him."*

—Jerry Vale

within the program. Part of an old Broadway evening that was called 'An Evening with Nichols and May' twenty-five years ago. An evening with Mike Nichols and Elaine May. Their technique was never to write down one single line, nothing on paper—very creative young people, everything improvised, everything ad-libbed from audience suggestions. And the reviewers loved them! They were very sharp and talented and creative people. Down Broadway's Memory Lane with Nichols and May. Somebody in the audience, on this particular night, yelled out, 'Disc jockey.'

■

"That, my friends, was called 'Nine O'clock Theatre' back in the 1950s, the fabulous fifties, presented by Alexander Cohen. And there we gave you two of America's leading satirists, Mike Nichols and Elaine May when they were improvising scenes, doing literary styles ranging from Batman and Robin to Plato. That particular vaudeville-type sketch was entitled 'Disc Jockey.' They prospered for awhile, then separated and the team was no longer. People often ask me if they were married. Yes, they were, but not to each other.
"I've got a team that was married. Shirley Jones and Jack Cassidy over WOR in New York City. The springtime quality, that delightful quality of the late Jack Cassidy and his wife Shirley Jones. And speaking of love, how about 'Vienna, My City of Dreams.'

■

"Ah, what a mood, and what an accompaniment by Percy Faith. The late and wonderful Percy Faith. 'Vienna, My City of Dreams.' I would call that warm hearted, the youth and beauty of Shirley Jones and Jack Cassidy.
"Joe Franklin, doing the Memory Lane party. The program known as 'don't throw your past away—you might need it someday.' For example, right now as we recall Jack Cassidy and Shirley Jones—in happier days, 'I'll Follow My Secret Heart.'

■

"They were lovely and attractive people, and memories do endure. Now back to old-time Las Vegas, when the big attraction, the biggest superstar on those stages, was a young man named Johnnie Ray.
"Hoping we haven't worn out the welcome mat. Once more, for your approval, these tunes.
("I Went Walking Down by the River. . . ." "If Your Sweetheart Sends a Letter of Goodbye.")
"There was a superstar, Johnnie Ray in Las Vegas. This is Joe Franklin doing the party with the entertainment dedicated to the disenfranchised among us, which includes, I think, about half the population of the USA. I'm with you strolling through Memory Lane with the young lady who gets the most requests week in and week out, Vera Lynn. Dame Vera Lynn, selling so many millions of copies of 'We'll Meet Again.'

*Johnnie Ray and
Miss Georgia Gibbs,
1957,* **$10-15.**

Vera Lynn, 1961,
$5-10.

Dame Vera Lynn with Joe.

"A lady who made wartime history, my friends. A British artist supreme and one of the most important singers certainly of all time. We're doing Vera Lynn—Dame Vera Lynn over Memory Lane, over WOR in New York, Joe Franklin hosting.

"And this was the lady, the lady we remember with great affection. Her efforts to bring comfort and joy and a touch of home to those millions of servicemen and women all over the world cannot be forgotten. And the songs she sang have become without any doubt an important slice of wartime history, with countless memories wrapped around the magical message of so many of those classics. One of them had to be one of the special songs with a special niche. Dame Vera Lynn back in the days when she was just Vera Lynn. Introducing 'The White Cliffs of Dover.'

■

"This is Joe Franklin on the star of New York, 710 AM WOR, the station with a heart. The station that really communicates.

"A bit of trivia: Years ago, there was a man on radio called Wendell Hall. He was called the red-headed music-maker and he had a song called 'Trickin' Pickin' a Slick Slick Chicken'!

"And now I give you Bob Hope's long-ago sidekick, the man with the mighty mustache, Jerry Colonna. Jerry Colonna doing a medley of songs that will live as long as there's music. If you're a teenager or an old-ager, you will love this song-acade. Why don't we sing along for awhile with the great, the mighty mustache, Jerry Colonna.

Jerry Colonna and Joe.

"The medley reminds me of the good old days, or rather the good old nights when friends and neighbors would gather 'round the family piano—or someone's piano—singing and dancing to the popular music of the day. Each song that Jerry Colonna sang during that medley sold over one million copies in sheet music alone! That's without phonograph records. Those were the hits—those were the days.

"How about a few minutes now called 'Big Band Revisited.' How about starting with the man who played the sweetest trumpet in the world, the late and wonderful Charlie Spivak, his orchestra, and a vocal by Gary Stevens. I would say about forty-three to forty-four years ago, 'My Devotion.'

■

"This is your party. That was perfectly beautiful, beautifully perfect— Charlie Spivak, 'My Devotion.' And we're saluting the Big Band era with Kay Kaiser and 'Slow Boat to China.'

■

"From 1932, fifty-two years ago, James Melton's recording of 'Only Make Believe.'

"We are in the midst of a rich segment of Americana. Songs from *Showboat.* That was the first one and there is one more, coming up right now. 'Showboat,' written by Jerome Kern and Oscar Hammerstein II. Recorded in 1932. Now get ready for a historical first. This was the very first record album ever devoted to songs from a single Broadway score—the first album ever built around a Broadway show. Greats on 78s to say the least. A very popular radio team that year was Frank Munn, the Golden Voice of Radio, and Countess Albani. This was their recording of 'Why Do I Love You' from *Showboat.*

■

Kay Kaiser, 1948,
$10-15.

*Joe at a recent
lecture.*

"And there, my friends, for a gorgeous finale, we had two of those immortal Kern and Hammerstein songs from *Showboat* recorded back in 1932, recorded by Frank Munn and Countess Albani, with orchestra conducted by Victor Young.

"This is Joe Franklin saying have a wonderful weekend. Remember, don't drive and drink, don't drink and drive. We'll meet again next week, same time, same place. Together we'll be turning back the hands of time, rolling back the sands of time."

3
Silents, Talkies, and Television

Charlie Chaplin, 1916,
$35-45.

Shortly after beginning his first radio show, Joe was biking among four different radio stations, doing a total of fourteen shows a week under the titles of "Vaudeville Isn't Dead," "Antique Record Shop," and "Echoes of the Big Time."

Having established a reputation on radio, Joe received a call from the old WJZ (now WABC) TV station in New York City. At that time, Channel 7 was on the air from 5 p. m. until midnight, but the station managers were considering adding some daytime shows—including an hour with Joe.

When they asked Joe what type of show he's like to do, he suggested a program in which people would talk to one another—an interview show. "I envisioned coming on with my idol, Eddie Cantor," Joe says, "and other people I admired who had been on my radio show. The people at the station thought I was out of my mind. They said, 'It's *television,* Joe—you've gotta give the audience *vision.* It's *vision.* You can't talk. There's no future in that. You've gotta give them *action*—pratfalls, slapstick, baggy pants, and seltzer bottles.'"

"Okay," Joe said, "Well, if I can't do a talk show, how about a program of kids dancing to phonograph records? (Rock and roll was just breaking in at that time.) I was told that no one would watch kids dancing to records. So who comes along? Dick Clark! Then I suggested a program with the words of old-time songs on the screen. They told me it was too corny. So who comes along? Mitch Miller."

Typically ahead of his time, Joe defied the station's objections and did a talk show after all. At first called simply "The Joe Franklin Show," the name changed to "Joe Franklin's Memory Lane" in honor of a 1924 movie called *Memory Lane,* a favorite radio theme song by the same name, and a chapter from the book *Great Laughter* that was called, "A Long Bunch of Memory Lanes."

To capitalize on his show's new title, Joe decided to integrate old movies with his interviews. The station wanted slapstick, so Joe gave it to them by buying every old movie he could find. Using the hunting techniques of his record days, he haunted antiques and junk shops, basements of old movie theatres, camera stores, and storage rooms. Within one year, Joe had purchased close to thirty thousand reels—mostly comedies—including films with such stars as Fatty Arbuckle, Ben Turpin, Charlie Chaplin, Ethel Merman, Rudy Vallee, and Bob Hope.

"At that time," says Joe, "everybody was in the stock market—not in the film market. But films were my investment—my antiques and collectibles.

"Eventually, the market for nostalgia came along, and there I was waiting in the wings. I amassed records for my radio show and I amassed early films with the same fervor. It felt natural to do something on television that had already worked for me on radio."

Not only has Joe collected the early films, but he has been instrumental in their preservation, as well. "In the old days, they never preserved their movies," says Joe. "They had no foresight. So much of what is rare, even at this moment, is crumbling and decomposing into dust and nothingness."

Originally, the movies were printed on nitrate film, which was highly combustible and caused numerous projection booth fires that were responsible for burning down theaters and killing thousands of movie-goers. In order to preserve his prints, Joe transfers the negatives onto safety film.

Joe Franklin/Memory Lane.

Lillian Gish, 1921,
$10-15.

Fatty Arbuckle,
$20-25.

Because of Joe's extensive collection, he now receives inquiries from cable television companies who want to rent his one-of-a-kind films. But sometimes even Joe can't help them out. "Marguerite Clark was the second most popular actress in the silent days. There isn't one existing print in the world, to the best of my knowledge, of a Marguerite Clark movie. Not one! There are works of art around from two thousand years ago, but we don't have one of her movies left. That's why film preservation is so important."

49

*Al Jolson in a scene
from the first talkie,
The Jazz Singer,
1928,* **$30-40.**

*This is the very first screen kiss from 1896, when it was considered risqué.
The players were May Irwin and John C. Rice.*

Rudolph Valentino,
$10-15.

Joe remembers the movies

Silent movies and "talkies." The pioneer films mean a great deal to me. The silents are the most interesting of films and come from the most interesting era of film. Of equal interest is that period when the talkies took over, but the technology was still experimental. We knew they had to have a microphone somewhere to pick up the dialogue. And the microphones were big and clumsy. You can spot them if you look carefully. They hid the microphones behind potted plants or the heroine would be gazing into her lover's eyes and whispering sweet nothings—to the mike bobbing from the ceiling."

For Joe the golden age of movies was from 1928 to about 1934. During this time the movie commercial was developed. It was much like TV commercials of today. Metropolitan Industrial Pictures and Audio Cinema were just two of the companies producing motion picture commercials. Joe adores the names of obscure or lesser known studios. For him they're a real turn on. The golden era commercial was a two-reeler that cost up to $2,000. According to Joe, "You can't even buy prime time on TV for that small an amount, but in those years it was big bucks. Automobile makers like Chrysler and Chevrolet used these motion pictures as did Coca-Cola, Westinghouse and many major corporations who do the very same thing today on television."

Charlie Chaplin,
1925, **$40-50.**

Norma Shearer, 1932,
$10-15.

Clark Gable, 1933,
$15-20.

    Some of the actors seen in industrial films include Dorothy Gulliver, Eddie Woods, and Otis Harlan. And such films are in Joe's library.

    Of all the major studios of the golden era MGM (Metro Goldwyn Mayer) was the largest. On their payroll in 1932, were Joan Crawford, Jean Harlow, Helen Hayes, Norma Shearer, Greta Garbo, Jackie Cooper, Marie Dressler, Jimmy Durante, Wallace Beery, Ramon Navarro, Buster Keaton, and Clark Gable, to name a few. Stars like Harlow and Gable were making approximately $2,500 a week, and Durante and Keaton about $1,000. MGM produced up to forty pictures a year during the golden era. Some of the most successful are Joe's favorites, and they include *Min and Bill, Trader Horn, Susan Lenox, The Champ, Tarzan of the Apes,* and *Grand Hotel* starring Greta Garbo. The resources of MGM were invested in enhancing the Garbo legend. When she appeared in her first talkie, *Anna Christie,* the slogan, "Garbo Talks" filled the ad space. And when she appeared in her first comedy, *Ninotchka,* the ad screamed "Garbo Laughs."

Greta Garbo, 1938,
$30-35.

*Wallace Beery and
Marie Dressler in* Min
and Bill, 1933, **$25-35.**

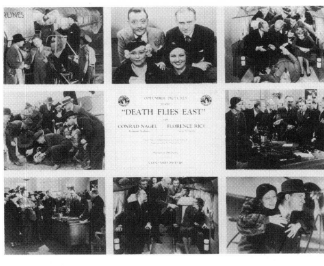

*Conrad Nagel,
back row, right,
1935, $35-45.*

*Frankie Darrow and
Lyle Talbot, 1936,
$15-25.*

"B" movies. "The poverty row studios that turn me on are just as important as the majors. Names like Invincible Pictures, Chesterfield Tower, Astor, Grand National, Monogram, with stars like Frankie Darrow and Kane Richmond—mostly people who had been in the major picture category once but missed out and they wound up in quickies. During the golden age, they would say, 'Don't make it good. Make it fast!'

"Sometimes I get together with fellow collectors and we have fun exchanging odd movie titles. I've got a vault of obscure films—pictures with Conrad Nagel, who had been a big star once and went into cheapies. But they had great fun making those pictures because they were kind of tongue in cheek. They were good actors who had Shakespearean backgrounds and they were doing rock bottom, kind of corny, quick movies. It's fun to watch them and know that they were putting the whole world on."

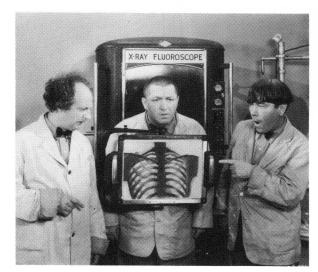

*The Three Stooges,
Larry, Curly, and Moe,
1938,* **$30-40.**

*Mr. and Mrs. William
Boyd (Hopalong Cas-
sidy), 1951, (Mrs.
Boyd is former ac-
tress Grace Bradley),*
$10-15.

A Few of Joe Franklin's favorite "B" movies

The Eleven Commandments
The Gold Racket
Navy Spy
Bank Alarm
Yellow Cargo
House of Secrets
Mud and Sand (a satire of Rudolph Valentino's *Blood and Sand*)
The Shriek (a take-off from *The Shiek*)
The Lighter That Failed (from *The Light That Failed*)
What Price Pants (from *What Price Glory*)
Violent Is the Word for Curly (a Three Stooges version of *Violent Is the Word
    for Carrie*)

56

Tex Ritter, **$10-15.**

"B" westerns. "The 'B' westerns are movies which I love and adore. When I was very young, I pretended that I was the Lone Ranger. I pictured myself on the screen or I acted out scenes from the radio programs (especially during school recess). I often think about how much today's generation is missing. How many youngsters in elementary school know that Roy Rogers is more than a place to order burgers, or that Gene Autry is more than the owner of the California Angels? How many youngsters realize that these were the world's best-known singing cowboys?

"The 'B' westerns have an enduring quality. Many of the heroes were accomplished stuntmen, like Ken and Kermit Maynard. They actually jumped off roofs into the saddle! They would dive for a gun across a splintered wooden floor while the fuse on the keg of gunpowder hissed in the background. They would really grab an overhanging tree limb at full gallop.

"I have had the pleasure of seeing my early idols of the "B" Westerns come on my TV show and prove in person that their movie personalities weren't a sham. In fact, the boyhood image I had built of them were only reinforced and strengthened as I met them in the flesh. There were Tex Ritter, Tim McCoy, Sunset Carson, William Boyd (Hopalong Cassidy), Roy Rogers and Dale Evans, and of course Gene Autry. They were all excellent guests.

"You know, Tom Mix, William S. Hart, Gene Autry, William (Hopalong Cassidy) Boyd, were solid men, dressed in leather and embroidery that were the business suits of the old West. Buster Crabbe was the first baby-faced cowboy, unlike those I just mentioned who had faces of granite and years of experience etched on their foreheads. Another of my favorite cowboys was Jonny Mack Brown.

The women of the western movies all seem to have their first blush of womanhood. Marsha Hunt in *Desert Gold,* Fay Wray in *The Conquering Horde,* Jean Arthur in *The Plainsman,* Joan Bennett in *The Texans,* Laraine Day in *Arizona Legend.* These young actresses got their first chance in westerns. If you look at the stills you'll see the stylish hairdos of the 1930s and a farm fresh manner.

Tex Ritter as Joe's guest.

Roy Rogers and Dale Evans, The Chevy Show, NBC-TV, February 22, 1952, **$10-15.**

Gene Autry

Buck Jones, 1922,
$20-25.

BUSTER CRABBE

From The New York Theatre—Home of the Westerns, *a booklet featuring western/cowboy stars. Here we see Buster Crabbe, whom many of us associate with Flash Gordon.*

Johnny Mack Brown in Law and Order, **1947, $10-15.**

"'B' westerns didn't pursue violence for its own sake. Bandits crumpled under a fusillade of .45 slugs, but the camera didn't linger on the wound. It was left to our imagination to know what a bullet does, just as we didn't have to see a close-up of sexual intercourse to know what went on after the hero and heroine rode into the sunset.

"Imagination is the key. The dirt and the saddle blankets were real, but the violence and sex were sanitized. Perhaps those filmmakers realized that sex and violence were extremely sensitive weapons to introduce into such a young medium."

Tom Mix, 1919,
$30-40.

Gary Cooper in High
Noon, **$10-15.**

Gary Cooper, Jane Darwell, and Cecil B. De Mille, Northwest Mounted Police, **$30-40.**

Gary Cooper, 1930, **$10-15.**

Serious westerns. "Serious westerns of the 1950s, such as *High Noon, Shane,* and *Bad Day at Black Rock* took westerns in a new direction. The happy endings were gone. The productions became flawless and the reality was drained out of them. You knew that Kirk Douglas and Burt Lancaster couldn't really ride hell-bent for leather in *Gunfight at the OK Corral.* To me, the most pleasing elements of the 'A' Westerns were the bits of 'B' movies that crept in, such as the towering heroics of Gary Cooper in *High Noon.*"

*Joe interviewing
Ginger Rogers.*

*Joe accepting the Humanitarian Award for Man of the Year.. At the podium
is Joey Adams, and beside him is Kate Smith.*

Joe with one of his all-time favorites—Conrad Nagel.

Gloria Swanson, a special guest.

Joe with Georgie Jessel.

Lobby card,
Strike Me Pink, *starring Eddie Cantor,*
1935, **$40-50.**

Lobby card, Special Delivery,
a Paramount silent film starring Eddie Cantor,
1927, **$175-200.**

Early theatre programs, **$5-50.**

Modern theater programs (souvenir books), **$10-35.**

What's On The Air, *a magazine for radio listeners, March 1930, cover photo of Amos 'n' Andy,* **$50-75.**

Lobby card, If You Knew Susie, *1948,* **$35-50.**

Lobby card, Eddie Cantor starring in Roman Scandals, **$35-50.**

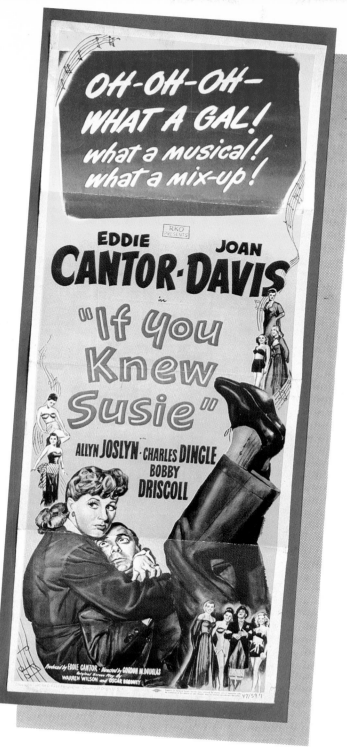

Poster, If You Knew Susie, *starring Eddie Cantor and Joan Davis, 1948,* **$50-75.**

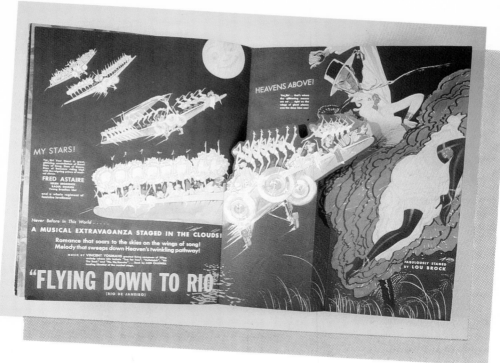

The interior of the RKO Radio Pictures announcement book, with pop up, Flying Down to Rio *starring Fred Astaire, 1933,* **$3000 plus.**

Shirley Temple storybook, **$150-175.** *Tim McCoy,* On the Mohawk Trail, *a Big Little Book,* **$25-35.**

Uncle Don record album, **$25-35.**

Albums filled with cigarette cards picturing the stars, $150-200.

4
Joe's TV and Movie Favorites

Jack Benny (impersonating Gracie Allen) and Al Jolson, October 25, 1948, $25-35.

The list of Joe's favorite performers is so all-encompassing that it could fill several volumes on its own. The personalities described in this chapter are included in Joe's new one-hour pilot for television, called "Joe Franklin's Hollywood Memories."

Jack Benny. "He portrayed a tightwad, but in private life, he was the opposite. He was generous to a fault. On his first radio appearance in 1932, guesting with Ed Sullivan, he said modestly, 'Ladies and gentlemen, this is Jack Benny. There will now be a slight pause while everybody asks, who cares?' But they did care. He got his own comedy show, and the rest is history."

Jack Benny and Rochester, 1940, **$15-20.**

Milton Berle, February 13, 1953, **$20-25.**

Milton Berle. This phenomenal star dominated TV from 1948 to 1956, as he wrote, directed, starred in, produced, composed, organized, and cast his own shows.

Berle's career began at age five when he won a contest for his impersonation of Charlie Chaplin. Within a few years, he had appeared in Chaplin's *Tillie's Punctured Romance,* and *Easy Street.*

74

Milton Berle with Little Ruthie Gilbert. Her famous line was, "It's bigger than both of us!" 1953, **$20-25.**

According to Joe, Berle had perfected his comedy style by the mid-1920s. Touring with the Keith-Albee vaudeville circuit, he became a master at putting down hecklers. And because he used material from other comedians, he developed a reputation of stealing jokes, even though he edited the gags to fit his own style.

When Berle appeared on Joe's show a few years ago, Joe asked him how he came to be called Uncle Miltie. This was Berle's reply:

"The phrase 'Uncle Miltie' came about by accident during the third year of the Texaco Star Theatre. Mothers and fathers, aunts and uncles, grandmothers and grandfathers would all approach me on the street. They used to say, 'Look, you're keeping our kids up. They watch you from 8 to 9 p. m. and then they stay up and they can't get up for school the next day. Could you please tell them to go to sleep?'

"I couldn't do that because of the FCC. But I said I'd keep it in mind. The third year started, and we hired a new script girl. When you're doing a variety show, or any kind of show, you have to know how much time you have left toward the end of the show and you've got to get off at a certain time because of the commercial value. The girl said, after we got through with the dress rehearsal, that we needed four more minutes. So we cut four minutes out of the script.

"It was a live show. In those days, you got what you saw, you saw what you got. There was no editing, there was no laugh track, there weren't any applause signs. There were no cue cards and there weren't any teleprompters. There was no videotape, no editing at all. If you made a mistake, you blew it!

"The first show of the third season started. At the end of the show, I was supposed to say goodnight and go into my theme song—'Near You.' As I got to that, there was a man under the camera who motioned to me that I needed seven more minutes. The girl had given us the wrong count.

"I had to ad-lib seven minutes. That's like a lifetime if you're a comic or comedian and you're ready to sign off and you haven't got any more material left in the show that's been planned. Now I was fishing and floundering, and a thought came into my mind. I said, 'Oh, by the way, I want to speak to you kids who are watching the show. I've been listening to some of your mothers and fathers and aunts and uncles. And the first thing I would like to tell you children is that there isn't anymore television after nine o'clock.' I said, 'I'm just kidding! But you listen to me—you get to bed early, right after the show is over, because you have to get up and go to school in the morning.'

"I didn't want to say, "Listen to *Mister* Berle,' or 'Listen to Milton.' I said, 'Listen to your Uncle Miltie.' I just said it. And the show ended.

"The following day, I went up to Boston to do a benefit for the Catholic Youth Organization, the CYO. They gave me a parade in the street, and as we were passing, two guys wearing hard hats, digging, said, 'Hi, Uncle Miltie!' We drove a couple of blocks more, and two children in the street said, 'Hi, Uncle Miltie!' And that was it."

During that same interview on Joe's show, Joe asked Berle what it had been like doing the weekly "Texaco Star Theatre."

"I directed, produced, oversaw—I was a pain in the bleep bleep. In those days, when I first went on television, I think I knew as much about producing or directing a television show as did the next guy. And my type of show was a revue, with a stand up single, a production number, and so forth.

"I had quite a lot of experience in vaudeville and Broadway shows, and I took the reins. We didn't have today's facilities and I was a pain. But it was an imperative pain. I was a disciplinarian. I was and still am a perfectionist, but it comes under the heading of dedication. Sometimes I was so overly meticulous that, if I was good or funny, I could have been better. I could have been better because my mind was not centered on my own work. I was worried about lighting, cameras, lenses, props, line delivery. Maybe if I was good—and I was fairly good—I could have been better with my own performance. I was thinking about other things, from Sid Stone's pitchman routine to little Ruthie Gilbert's lines."

According to Joe, "Milton dominated his medium, the television screen, the same way Charlie Chaplin dominated motion pictures. I think the reason that Berle isn't on TV today is because nobody has thought to ask him. And that deprives the American public—the world public—of being entertained by a master."

Fanny Brice. "Long after her passing, she became a legend all over again as *Funny Girl,* portrayed on stage and screen by Barbara Streisand. Fanny was unquestionably the world's most popular comedienne. Her hilarious heyday was 1922 to 1932. She was a dynamo. Later on, her characterization of Baby Snooks brought her to number one in the radio ratings. I can still hear her catch phrase, 'Why, Daddy?' "

Joe E. Brown. "He was a monarch of comedy. Either you loved him or you had no feelings for him. He was like the Three Stooges. He either warmed you or he chilled you. His colleagues on the Warner Brothers lot included

Fanny Brice as Baby Snooks (Toasties Time), 1939, **$15-20.**

Joe E. Brown, 1933, **$25-35.**

George Raft, Paul Muni, James Cagney, and Bette Davis. And even with such stiff competition, his baseball parodies, and his comedies in general, out-grossed every other kind of film on that great Warner Brothers lot. Joe E. Brown was at the height of his powers in 1928. Today he is almost forgotten."

77

Left to right: announcer Harry Von Zell, producer Vic Knight, songstress Dinah Shore, Eddie Cantor, and composer Edgar Fairchild at the piano, 1941, **$35-45.**

Eddie Cantor and Deanna Durbin, 1937, **$50-75.**

Eddie Cantor. To Joe Franklin, Eddie Cantor was not only a favorite comedian and entertainer, but his first friend in show business. Joe attended Cantor's radio show every Sunday night, until he knew the theme song, "I Love to Spend Each Sunday with You," backwards and forwards. And when Joe was seventeen years old, he was hired to script a radio program called "Ask Eddie Cantor," for which Joe provided the records and memorabilia.

According to Joe, Cantor's list of protégés is long and impressive: George Burns and Gracie Allen; Bobby Breen; Bert Gordon, the Mad Russian; Deanna Durbin; Dinah Shore; Eddie Fisher; Sammy Davis, Jr.; and Joan Davis.

"I'll tell you one thing about Eddie," Joe says of his favorite, "He was the only entertainer ever, an amazing statistic, to be Number One, not Two, but One, in radio, movies, TV, burlesque, vaudeville, Broadway musical comedy, recordings. You name it, he was Number One.

Eddie Cantor and his wife Ida, 1933.

Eddie Cantor and Joe Franklin when Joe was writing Eddie's show.

Eddie Cantor with Joe Franklin and his wife Lois.

Eddie Cantor and Eddie Fisher, June 16, 1954, **$40-50.**

"Eddie Cantor was affectionately nicknamed 'Banjo Eyes.' He had those big saucer banjo eyes that set the mood for his whole personality—bright and dazzling and sparkling. I think Eddie is mostly remembered by his trademark, the way he sang, that frantic delivery, clapping his hands and bouncing up and down on the stage, waving his handkerchief, sort of dashing and darting back and forth with feverish pace, which legend has began one night way downtown, in NYC, in an amateur night contest. As a means of avoiding the objects being thrown on stage by the audience, Eddie developed his unique style. He is also associated with dozens of songs, one of which is titled 'Ida.' Ida was his childhood sweetheart who later became his wife. Every chance he got he would sing 'Ida,' which of course he would dedicate to his lovely wife.

"Eddie was the first entertainer to be seen nationwide via the coaxial cable. He appeared on the 'Colgate Comedy Hour,' 1950, and paved the way for such entertainers as Jack Benny, Bob Hope, Jimmy Durante, et al. You could say that in the early days of television he was a pioneer, a pioneer in a new medium, one which many entertainers were afraid to participate in.

"I have a few favorite Cantor stories. One about a birthday cake. Eddie had five daughters, and one complained about the strawberries on her birthday cake being too small. Eddie responded by saying that he didn't have any strawberries when he was a kid. His daughter said, 'Aren't you lucky to be living with us.'

"I once told Eddie a joke and he said, 'Joe, that's the kind of joke that not only closed theaters—it closed cities!'

Eddie "Banjo Eyes"
Cantor, 1953, **$35-45.**

Eddie and Joan Da-
vis in Show Busi-
ness, **$20-25.**

82

Samuel Goldwyn presents EDDIE CANTOR in "THE KID FROM SPAIN"
with Lyda Roberti
UNITED ARTISTS PICTURE   Made in U. S. A.

Eddie Cantor in The Kid from Spain, *1934,* **$25-35.**

Irving Berlin and Eddie Cantor. 1941, **$40-50.** *Eddie sang Berlin's "Any Bonds Today."*

*Eddie Cantor and
Joan Davis in* If You
Knew Susie, **$20-25.**

*Eddie Cantor and
Joan Davis in* How to
Win Damsels and In-
fluence Girls, *1943,*
$20-25.

Eddie Cantor and Sophie Tucker, 1936, $40-50.

Eddie Cantor as Maxie the Taxi on "The Colgate Comedy Hour," 1951, $35-45.

"In 1950 I produced an evening called 'My Forty Years in Show Business,' at Carnegie Hall. It was SRO (standing room only) with three hundred in the back and two hundred on stage. Eddie was fifty-eight and we walked to the stage door where an old man was waiting. He said, 'Mister Cantor, I've been a great, great fan of yours since I was a kid.' 'How old are you?' Eddie asked. 'I'm ninety, Mister Cantor. The real reason I'm here is that I'd give anything to see the show and it's sold out.' Eddie offered to get him a place standing in the back. 'Man, I've got varicose veins,' the old man cried. 'Maybe you could get me tickets to Sonja Henie, at the Garden?' That's what Cantor called "chutzpah" and he laughed so hard he almost burst a vocal cord.

"After the show Eddie and I had a drink backstage. Among the many celebrities that were backstage were Harry Richman (who sounded much like Al Jolson), Milton Berle, the late and great Jack Benny, Kate Smith and Ted Collins, Ruth Etting, Belle Baker, many politicians, and Sophie Tucker. Sophie came up to Eddie and said, 'I have three sponsors who want me for a radio series. Two sponsors who want me for a TV series. Three movie companies are bidding for a movie on my life. Four record labels are fighting to get me, and six supper clubs in NYC alone are competing for me.' Eddie patted her on the shoulder and said, 'Don't worry, Sophie, you'll get something soon.'

Charlie Chaplin in The Gold Rush, *1924,* **$15-20.**

"Eddie Cantor," says Joe, "was the man who really helped America and the whole world laugh their worries away when they had Depression troubles. He was the right man at the right time. He was also politically minded. He once lost a sponsor because he was so outspoken about the nonchalant attitude prevailing in regard to the impending outbreak of World War II. Eddie ended his evening by expressing his political views, and this caused him to be pulled off the air for two years or so. He was to his time what Mort Sahl was to the 1960s—a conscience."

Charlie Chaplin. This king of silent comedy made thirty-four shorts and one full-length feature before starting his own production company. From that company came such classics as *The Gold Rush, City Lights,* and *Modern Times.* Doing what he did best, Chaplin continued to produce silent movies into the 1930s, even though sound tracks had been used for years.

"I've heard people on radio and television," Joe says, "who analyze and scrutinize and try to intellectualize Chaplin. People have tried to look into the Freudian significance and all the shading and interpretations of Chaplin's comedy. I had Charlie Chaplin on my radio show once. And I asked him what he thought about these people who write thick volumes analyzing Chaplin films, suggesting that every time he kicks the fat man in the behind he's supposed to be knocking the Establishment.

"He answered, 'Joe, all I wanted to do was to make people laugh. All these people are analyzing what wasn't there in the first place.' He swore that to me. And he surely must have known."

Bing Crosby, 1937,
$20-30.

Bing Crosby. Joe describes his 1976 interview with Bing Crosby as "the only time I melted." Bing was in New York for a three-week engagement being staged for charity. His appearance on Joe's show was meant to be a ten-minute plug. But he ended up singing to the cameramen, joshing his wife about their courtship, and talking candidly about his life.

JF: I was on a Memory Lane cruise and I have to give you one name. He's no longer with us, sadly, but he always spoke about you and the Belvedere Hotel. His name was Sid Gary.

BC: Sid Gary was the master of the double talk. Did you know him? He was the best, the greatest. He had a real professorial appearance. He dressed like he was going down to Wall Street. There used to be a house detective at the Belvedere Hotel. He was an Irishman and wore a green derby. And any time we'd come in from a cafe or restaurant late at night, Sid would give him about fifteen minutes of double talk. And he'd just keep you yessing, saying "Yes, sir, Mr. Gary," and he didn't understand a word Sid said. Sid was also a great singer, with a big voice. He did "The Road to Mandalay"— big, epic-type songs.

JF: Bing, there was once a battle of the baritones on the radio—you opposite Russ Columbo. Had Russ Columbo lived, would he have been as popular as you are?

Bing Crosby and Joe.

BC: He was a handsome guy. He had a warm, ingratiating personality. And he could sing and was a good musician. He played wonderful violin. I think that, had he lived, he would have been a big romantic star. At the Coconut Grove in Los Angeles, Russ and I sang some duets and quintets with the Rhythm Boys. He was going with Carole Lombard, a beautiful woman with a great personality. She was crazy about him. They would have been married, I'm sure, if he hadn't been killed.

JF: Sad, mysterious death.

BC: It was. I know the facts, but it's probably a little gruesome and I wouldn't want to repeat them. His mother—it was an Italian family and he had three brothers—had a serious heart condition. They never told her about Russ's death. They wrote her letters and had them mailed from London, from Italy, saying he was on tour. And she died a year-and-a-half later without ever knowing that he had been killed. They were sure that if she had been told, she would have died immediately.

JF: You must have sold more records than anybody else.

BC: I think the Beatles sold more or came close. These days, there are more record buyers, stereos. In the old days, if you got a record to sell 100,000, that was a big sale. I have to check and see if I got paid for all those records. It's hard to believe I sold forty million records. I didn't get that much money, Joe!

Bing Crosby, 1937,
$20-30.

Bing Crosby, Bob
Hope, and Dorothy
Lamour in Road to
Rio, 1947, **$10-15.**

Another scene from
Road to Rio, **$10-15.**

JF: The fellows who impersonated you in vaudeville, including Sid Gary, always sang "Buh-buh-buh-boo." Did you really say it? They say Cary Grant never said "Judy, Judy, Judy." Humphrey Bogart never said, "All right, Louie, drop the gun." Did Bing Crosby really go "Buh-buh-buh-boo." when he sang?

BC: Yes, there are a couple of records—"Learn to Croon" from the picture *College Humor.*

JF: Was that on purpose?

BC: It was considered very classy. There was "Voh-dee-o-do," "Hi-dee-ho," "Ha-cha-cha." But now the scat singers are fantastic. You take Ella Fitzgerald, Mel Torme, Cleo Lane. It's light years ahead of anything I did.

JF: Did you ever reject or turn down a song—not that you regretted later on, but something you could have had but turned down?

BC: I did a picture called *She Loves Me Not,* and we had a song in there called "Love in Bloom." I didn't like it. I sang it in the picture, did a record, and just kind of threw it away. It wound up as Jack Benny's theme song.

JF: The pairing of you and Hope and, of course, Dorothy Lamour, made it a trio. How did that start?

BC: Hope had his own radio show, and I did, too. We were pals from the Friars Club. He started kidding me one night and I kidded him, oh about his nose and his bad jokes. And we sort of developed a feud like Fred Allen and Jack Benny—make-believe. I was on his show and he was on mine, and the feud got funny. The head of Paramount said we should be together—a one-time shot. The first was *The Road to Singapore.* We had very tolerant directors that let us do what we wanted.

The program with Bing is still so popular that it is now printed in the black market. According to Joe, "That's because it was such a rare and touching experience not just for me, but for my audience. These are the kind of moments we treasure forever and ever."

Joan Davis. "One fantastically gifted comedienne who reached the height of her movie fame by appearing as Eddie Cantor's leading lady, was Joan Davis. I really miss her. And somehow I find it very difficult to think of Lucille Ball, or Carol Burnett, or Phyllis Diller or the many who followed without thinking to myself how much they must have been influenced by Joan Davis.

"Joe Franklin was the most important factor in Bing's New York engagement. He always supported Bing and me and made little ol' New York a very wonderful place."

—Kathryn Crosby

Joe interviewing Dorothy Lamour. During the interview Joe held up a still from his collection, showing Dorothy Lamour wearing her famous sarong.

Joan Davis, 1938, **$20-25.**

This photo was released to promote RKO Radio's musical comedy Show Business. *The caption reads, "Torridly illustrated. Joan Davis GETS HER MAN! The first such event, so far as oldtimers can recall, in her long film career. The lucky gentleman is Eddie Cantor, and the scene, in all of its electrifying entirety will be publicly unveiled in RKO Radio's musical comedy,* Show Business. *Can I TAKE it!" says Joan, 1943,* **$20-25.**

Jim Backus, 1965, **$5-10.**

She had a very popular TV series in the 1950s called 'I Married Joan.' Her co-star was Jim Backus. In the 1950s Jim Backus provided the off screen voice for the myopic cartoon character Mr. Magoo. His long running series included 'I Married Joan' and the still popular 'Gilligan's Island.'"

W. C. Fields, 1939,
$15-20.

W. C. Fields. "He continues to give pleasure," Joe says, "though he's been gone for many years. His tradition will never die, because he was a comedy master. I think I'm really and truly addicted to his type of humor. To me, W. C. Fields was much more than a cartoonlike character who would stroll through movies muttering asides and leaving a trail of chaos strewn behind him. To me, he was a way of life, creating a pathway of happiness for millions of Depression-weary Americans."

Walter Hampden. According to Joe, this successful and sensitive actor was always associated with his portrayal of Cyrano de Bergerac. When he was in the offices of a New York producer, looking for a TV role based on Cyrano, the receptionist asked who he was. Hampden introduced himself. Then, according to Joe, the secretary asked, "What have you done?" Without hesitation, Hampden replied, "To whom?"

Buster Keaton. Joe describes this classic comedian as "Hollywood's champion pie thrower. When he teamed up with Jimmy 'Shnozzola' Durante, even the most jaded moviegoers burst into gales of laughter."

Buster Keaton, 1924,
$20-25.

Keaton was also a talented stuntman, as were the other kings of silent comedy—Harold Lloyd, Harry Langdon, and Charlie Chaplin. At the climax of Keaton's *Hard Luck,* he had to dive off a sixty-foot-high platform. According to Joe, "The trick in Keaton's stunt was that he had to miss the pool and crash into the marble tiling—at least, a papier-mâché imitation of marble that would allow him to sink inexplicably into the earth.

"The stunt itself was going to be no mean feat, but Keaton got the shock of his life when he discovered, on looking down, that the imitation was so carefully done that he couldn't tell the difference between it and the real tile. Before he could decide what to do, a gust of wind pitched him over the edge and he made a mid-air evaluation of hard and soft surfaces. Ringed by an impression of bathing beauties, he plunged safely through the papier-mâché. To film buffs of today, it's just another zany Keaton finale. But the terror of a possibly fatal accident was accepted as a way of life by the pioneers of films."

Bert Lahr. "He has been called one of the funniest men in history, and I agree. He became famous by playing characters of heroic ineptitude—wildly, hopelessly incompetent. But it was as the Cowardly Lion in *The Wizard of Oz* that Bert Lahr won motion picture immortality. But he returned to Broadway and to radio with this remark: 'How many lion parts are there in Hollywood?' "

Stan Laurel. According to Joe, "Stan once told me that he wanted to write a book about Laurel and Hardy called *Two Minds Without a Single Thought.* Unfortunately, he never did. Audiences didn't watch Laurel and Hardy thinking they were geniuses—they just laughed and laughed. In my childhood, they were known affectionately as Fat and Skinny. Their kind of comedy will never go out of style. No matter where they are, I hope they know how beloved they still are."

Bert Lahr as The
Cowardly Lion, 1939,
$15-20.

Laurel and Hardy,
$25-35.

Laurel and Hardy in
the late 1940s,
$25-35.

Harold Lloyd in Safe-ty Last. *Lloyd is one of the geniuses of the art of silent comedy, along with Charlie Chaplin, Buster Keaton, and Harry Langdon.* **$20-25.**

Ed Wynn as "The Perfect Fool," 1929, **$25-35.**

Harold Lloyd. "A genial, bespectacled man, he innovated a screen character with a great love of life. He had a sunny disposition telescoped in a winning smile. His income was second only to Charlie Chaplin's. He delivered what moviegoers ordered. His masterpiece was *Safety Last,* in which he portrayed a human fly clinging to the hand of a clock eleven floors above the street."

Ed Wynn. "He was known as the Perfect Fool, a role he created on Broadway in 1921. He was a funny man. Wynn was also a fine dramatic actor and won many awards, including the Emmy, for his fine performances. One of my favorite Ed Wynn inventions is the eleven-foot pole for people he wouldn't touch with a ten-foot pole."

5
"Franklinizing" the Stars

Shirley Temple, 1937,
$30-40.

Part of Joe Franklin's success must be attributed to his amazing memory for show business stories. Not only has he amassed an impressive collection of memorabilia, but he has the memories to go with each item. Joe can talk for hours about celebrities, so sit back and get acquainted with your favorite personalities as Joe "Franklinizes" these stars.

Shirley Temple Black. When this grown-up childhood star appeared on Joe's show, Joe tried to address her current interests—not nostalgia. But according to Joe, that lasted only a few minutes before he *had* to ask about her old movies.

"She was Shirley Temple to me," Joe says. "She told me that Santa Claus wanted her autograph when she was a child star, only six years of age. From there, we talked for the remainder of the program about her movies. Shirley told me that she was delighted with the collectibility of the 'new' Shirley Temple collectibles. She said she had no sad memories, that she never worked hard—it all seemed like play.

"About two weeks after that program, a large package was delivered to my office. It was an early-day Shirley Temple scrapbook, with clippings, photographs, and all kinds of collectible nostalgia. It is an absolutely priceless piece of film history! The note inside said it was for me to keep—a memento of our meeting. The Temple charm is still undeniable, and she is every inch a lady."

Humphrey Bogart and George Raft. "Few people know about the war of the shoes that went on between George Raft and Humphrey Bogart. George Raft was a dancer and multidimensional actor, but it bothered him that his tough-guy image was sometimes lessened by the height of his co-stars.

"In *Souls at Sea,* he was paired with Gary Cooper and had elevated shoes to top all elevated shoes especially made so he could almost match belt buckles with Cooper. Following this, he had no fears about playing opposite Humphrey Bogart. In the opening sequence of *Invisible Stripes,* they appeared together in a shower, and Bogart was at least half an inch shorter. In the next scene, both men appeared with their clothes and shoes on, and Bogart suddenly had an edge on Raft. Raft examined his co-star up and down. A smile tugged at Bogart's mouth when Raft saw that he was wearing well-built-up shoes.

George Raft, 1941,
$15-20.

98

Humphrey Bogart,
1955, **$30-35**.

George Raft in a candid with Cary Grant, 1972, **$35-45**.

Humphrey Bogart sporting a mustache, **$40-50.**

Humphrey Bogart, 1935, **$30-40.**

"Raft had been outdone that time, but the tables were soon to be turned. Their next film was the famous motion picture *Drive by Night*.

" 'It's a good thing nobody noticed how we changed height in that last movie,' Raft said good-naturedly to Bogart.

" 'Yeah, we're not growing boys anymore,' replied Bogie. But when they went on camera, Raft had put back into service the platform shoes he had worn with Cooper, and there he stood—at least a half inch taller than Bogart.

"I don't really know if these two superstars took themselves and their height all that seriously in private life. Perhaps they only thought it was important for their careers."

Jerry Colonna. Known as Bob Hope's sidekick, Colonna was to be honored at the famous Sardi's restaurant in New York. Hundreds of guests arrived, but the guest of honor couldn't be found. Vincent Sardi, owner of the restaurant, finally tracked down Colonna at the NBC studios, where Colonna was in the middle of a taping.

"Sardi spotted a mimic in the audience," Joe says, "and after a costume change, there was Jerry Colonna, mustache and all, on stage. The impromptu performance went on for almost half an hour, at the end of which only Sardi noticed the real Colonna doubled up in laughter at the back of the room."

Jerry Colonna, 1940,
$10-15.

*Abbott and Costello,
1953*, **$10-20.**

Lou Costello. According to Joe, Lou Costello's famous "I'm a b-a-a-a-d boy" line originated when he was caught smoking in the boys' room and was ordered to write "I'm a bad boy" on the blackboard one hundred times. "Halfway through," Joe says, "he couldn't resist filling a lull in the teacher's lecture by intoning his famous line, which years later he used in the act, and which is always associated with Abbott and Costello, just as we associate 'Who's on First' with this famous pair."

Kirk Douglas. "When you first meet Kirk Douglas in person, it is surprising to find that he is not as tall as one thinks he should be. He is not a six-footer. Yet his manner is so intense and his portrayals so powerful that fans think of him as a tall man. Dustin Hoffman, Al Pacino, Alan Ladd, Mickey Rooney, Edward G. Robinson, are just a few shorter stars. I had a conversation once with Billy Rose who was diminutive in size and he said, 'I'm taller than anybody I know when I stand on my wallet.'"

Joan Fontaine. "Many people don't know that Joan Fontaine and Olivia de Haviland are sisters. This story was related to Joe by Joan Fontaine during one of her appearances on Joe's show. Shortly after she made *Rebecca*, Joan Fontaine was invited to dinner at the Goldwyns'. Sam Goldwyn had a residence on a hilltop in Hollywood, and when movie stars received an invitation there, it meant they'd really made it. Joan Fontaine and her husband of the time, Brian Ahern, arrived at Goldwyns' in their elegant garb and fashionably late only to find that there were no cars in the driveway. They decided to drive around for awhile to kill time, but still no cars had appeared when they checked back. Brian thought they should return home to reread the invitation, thinking they may have had the wrong day. They went home and found the date and time were right. But by then they were an hour late. They made their way back to the Goldwyns quickly to find the Goldwyns still waiting for them—for dinner alone!

Joan Fontaine as Joe's guest.

Joe believes in giving equal time. Here is Joe interviewing Olivia de Havilland, Joan Fontaine's sister.

Greta Garbo, **$30-35.**

Greta Garbo. "Even though she hasn't made a movie in forty years, Garbo is still Garbo. Twice she was named best actress by the New York Film Critics for *Anna Karenina,* 1935, and for *Camille* in 1937. Amazingly, she never won an Academy Award—a situation remedied in 1954 when she received a special Oscar for her unforgettable screen performances.

"In 1941, following the release of *Two Faced Woman,* she announced her retirement from films. True to character, she never explained why. Not unrelated was the reception accorded *Two Faced Woman,* which was greeted as an unqualified disaster. The less communicative she became, the more the public clamored to hear about her and the more publicity was generated.

"She is, I guess, a recluse, living on the upper East Side of New York City, never giving any interviews. She goes to theaters where Garbo festivals are playing. I see her sitting quietly at the back of the theater wearing her slouch hat, and we exchange smiles and shake hands, but she declines to give interviews.

"The Greta Garbo mystique remains intact with new audiences discovering her in film festivals and on television. She captures them as she did her original and older fans. Without making a film since 1941, she is still the prototype of all stars."

104

Judy Garland, 1963,
$40-50.

Judy Garland. Joe's favorite story of this legendary performer occurred when Judy's daughter, Liza Minnelli, was starring in her first major role on Broadway. "Judy was down in the orchestra seats feeling exuberant because her daughter was doing so well. Liza was doing a song, and Judy could hardly contain herself. Before long, she could be heard humming the tune, then mouthing the lyrics, and finally she started singing out loud.

"Now, Garland really belted out a song. Her voice was drowning out Liza's. The audience, who had come to see Judy Garland's daughter, didn't enjoy Judy's emotion. Before the audience could be called unruly, Liza stopped and the theater was silent.

"'Would the young lady auditioning in the audience please hold off for the moment and come back for the casting call on Tuesday?' she said. The show ran through to the end without any more problems. After the final curtain, the woman in the front row ascended to the stage to give the audience an impromptu performance of mother and daughter singing 'Over the Rainbow.' That love between performers and audience, a mutual affair, is something I will always remember."

Fanny Hurst. This actress and novelist was not only Joe's first guest on his ahead-of-its-time TV talk show, she was also his source of inspiration and new ideas. Her brainstorming meetings with Joe in Central Park attracted other artists, including Dick Powell, Tony Martin, Rudy Vallee, Eartha Kitt, and others.

Joe best remembers Fanny for her calla lily trademark. "Fanny never appeared in public without a jeweled calla lily adorning her attire. She also drew this favorite flower on all her personal correspondence."

A scene from the 20th Century-Fox Production
"ROSE OF WASHINGTON SQUARE"

Al Jolson, 1939, **$30-40.**

Al Jolson. "Al Jolson was starring in the musical *Honeymoon Express* early in his career when he developed a serious ingrown toenail on his left foot. The pain was severe, and he was on the verge of leaving the show. Instead, he managed to relieve his pain by getting down on one knee halfway through the performance and pouring out his sentimental ballads with a great show of emotion. He later worked the technique into his famous 'Mammy' number, long after his ingrown toenail had healed.

"I knew Al Jolson for only a brief period of time. I found to my delight that he was far from being only the result of this gimmick. Vibrations came from his body—the only case in which I understood what people meant by 'good vibes.' "

Jack Lemmon. According to Joe, Jack arrived in New York with little money. He found a five-dollar-a-week room and a job playing piano in a beer hall that featured silent movies. But when he found that he wasn't making enough to even pay the rent, he agreed to take on the added job of a waiter.

Jack Lemmon, 1975,
$5-10.

"His boss," says Joe, "thought he would have a little fun at Jack's expense and asked him, on his first night as a waiter, if he would advise a guest that napkins should be tucked in under the chin. Seeing his tip flying out the window, Jack approached the table and inquired, "Pardon me, sir, but would you like a shave or a haircut?' Jack may have been back at the piano for the silent films the next night. He credits this experience with helping his comedy technique."

Bette Midler. A star who made early appearances on Joe's show, Bette Midler used to rummage through Joe's record collection for "campy" tunes. "When she found the 'Boogie Woogie Bugle Boy of Company B,' she had to hear it just because she thought the title was so different. Her rendition of this song is marvelous and Midler."

Robert Mitchum. "Robert Mitchum was in New York promoting a movie and arrived at my TV studio wearing tinted eyeglasses. On camera, I asked Robert Mitchum to remove the glasses. His response: 'No, Joe, I'd prefer leaving them exactly where they are.' I said, 'Bob, why won't you do me a favor and

Robert Mitchum,
1975, $4-8.

take them off?' As he started to fume, I continued, 'Only because our viewers want to see you better—your twinkling eyes and renowned grin and reactions as you reminisce with me. After all, we're on television, not radio.' After a tense moment or two, Bob removed the glasses and my audience got to see a real live Robert Mitchum and not the half hidden star who had appeared on a few other talk shows in New York that week."

Mabel Normand and Mack Sennet. In June of 1915, Mack Sennet, a top movie director noted today for the Keystone Cops, and Mable Normand, his leading lady, set a date to get married.

"Mabel was naive and Mack Sennet was a worldly, suave man. The bride to be asked Sennet to check out an old friend of hers who was having hard luck. They had been models in NYC. As the wedding day approached there were rumors that some model was after Sennet. Normand was advised to let him have his last fling. The rumors grew stronger and Mabel decided to talk to her old friend. After their talk Mabel was ashamed of herself. As she entered her own apartment, she realized that her handbag was missing. Thinking she had left it at her model friend's house, she telephoned but there was no answer. She decided to drive back and get her bag. There was no

Mack Sennett, 1916.
The autograph reads:
"For Mabel, All My
Love, Mack."
$400-500.

Mabel Normand,
1916, **$300-400.**

Mabel Normand,
1916, **$300-400.**

Conrad Nagel, 1924,
$35-45.

response to Mabel's knock. She went around the house and entered by the back door. She walked into the kitchen, then into the living room. No one was there. Mabel went upstairs. She heard Sennet's voice inside the bedroom. She opened the door.

"It was said that Mabel Normand repaired to a friend's house, that of Fatty Arbuckle, and lay as in a coma for three days. Flowers and messages appeared hourly from the distraught Sennet. Finally it was decided, through the intercession of friends, that Mabel's contract would be played out and that would be that. That WAS it. She died fifteen years later, the victim of hard living and maltreatment by her public and her profession."

Genel Fowler, in his biography of Mack Sennet, *Father Goose,* said of Normand, "She was an innate mimic, but could not imitate mental processes. Possibly she was an authentic genius. Perhaps Isadora Duncan was the only other woman of our time to possess beauty, charm, ability, soul, and courage the equal of Mabel's. And, like the gallant Isadora, Mabel walked with tragedy."

Will Rogers. Joe's favorite story about Will Rogers concerns his speech to a group of bankers. "The bankers were told that Rogers had a sour view of bankers, but they seemed not to mind this as long as they were entertained. Will Rogers began by saying, "You're as fine a group of gentlemen as ever foreclosed on a widow. I'm honored to be with you Shylocks.' The insults continued, and there was laughter. Of course, Rogers always addressed the audience by calling them 'gentlemen.' He was asked back!"

Kate Smith. When Joe first met Kate Smith in 1947, her ability to tell stories about herself that were both comical and emotional made a strong impression. Joe describes her as "ahead of her time, a women's libber, the singer's singer, radio's first lady, and the songbird of the South.

Kate Smith, 1932,
$30-40.

111

Kate Smith, 1932,
$30-40.

"In her book, *Upon My Lips*, says Joe, "Kate discussed two great embarrassments of her life. The first was that she never married. She said, 'There is a need for a different attitude on the part of society for the unmarried woman . . . a perfectly normal person, with the same wishes and ambitions as anyone. She merely fulfills them differently.'

"The other embarrassment was that some people thought she made her reputation on her weight as much as her singing. Her weight problem was difficult to deal with when she was first breaking into the business. Her first role was Tiny Little in *Honeymoon Lane*. When told that she had landed the part, she was ecstatic at first. The she realized that it was the role of a buffoon. She said, 'They told me my weight, then about 190 pounds, would be a handicap in my career, whereas I now had to acknowledge, to my dismay, that it had actually gotten me the part.'"

Barbra Streisand. Joe's television show has been a vehicle for rising stars, giving early exposure to such celebrities as Eddie Murphy, Don Rickles, Flip Wilson, Bernadette Peters, Bill Cosby, and Joan Rivers. Another superstar who made several appearances on Joe's show before achieving celebrity status was Barbra Streisand.

Jimmy Stewart, **$5-10.**

"She used to camp out in my office," says Joe. "She dressed offbeat and looked a bit offbeat. But she seethed with talent. I remember when she came along with her very slow treatment of 'Happy Days Are Here Again.' This particular song was used by the Democrats during the Great Depression. She treated it without the bouncy nature so many of us are used to hearing. She heard that tune on one of my old, scratchy records and sensed the complexity of the lyrics. She is artistry at work."

Jimmy Stewart. "I seldom fall asleep at previews. But I once fell asleep at the preview of a Jimmy Stewart motion picture—seated next to Jimmy Stewart. I was embarassed! Then Jimmy nudged me. 'You didn't miss anything, partner,' he said. 'The best is yet to come.'"

Gwen Verdon. "During *Redhead* (which starred Gwen Verdon on Broadway) an entire set fell on her. The set had heavy jail bars, and they landed on her feet. Bob Fosse jumped over the orchestra pit to see if she was hurt. The producer of the show ran out on stage and frantically asked if there was a doctor in the house. When they finally carried her backstage five doctors came up from the audience, and all of them were psychiatrists!"

113

6
Shoppers' Guide

Rosemary Clooney,
$1-5.

The listings in this section will give you a bird's-eye view of the market for show business memorabilia. Because values and prices vary in different parts of the country, this section is a shopper's guide more than a price guide.

Values are based upon availability (rarity) and condition. They also are determined by provenance—the collection that housed a particular item.

For those readers who want to expand their knowledge and collections the author recommends the following publication: Joe Franklin's Memory Lane Catalog, Box 201, NY, NY 10021.

Singer Dick Haymes as Joe's guest.

Tony Bennett telling Joe about his talents as a painter.

Tiny Tim and Joe.

Dan Dailey and band-leader Ray Anthony (a Cary Grant look-alike).

Joe with Mickey Rooney and Gene Krupa.

All the memorabilia listed and illustrated in this book is from Joe Franklin's collection. Every item is in either mint condition or the best condition available. Joe tells us that, no matter how much he has accumulated, he constantly searches for an item that may complete a set or is considered nonexistent. The following are a few of the items for which Joe is still searching.

The original Broadway playbill for Al Jolson in *Bombo*, 1921, in mint condition.
The 11" × 14" title card to *Forty Little Mothers,* starring Eddie Cantor, 1940, in mint condition.
A pressbook for Jimmy Durante and Buster Keaton in *What, No Beer!,* 1933.
The LPs on the Dot label recorded in the 1950s by Bill Kenny, the lead tenor of the Ink Spots.
The sheet music for the production number of "March of the Doagies," which was deleted from the film *The Harvey Girls,* 1945.
A 78 RPM titled "I'll Never Smile Again," recorded on the Bluebird label by Elton Britte, a country-western singer.
The 1943 film *Hit Parade,* starring Susan Hayward and John Carroll.
The poster for *Sincerely Yours,* 1952, starring Liberace.

Records

Joe's advice to the novice record collector is simple. First, never allow trends to determine your purchases. Jazz records generally have the highest market value, but allow your personal taste in music to be your ultimate guide.

Second, purchase records in mint condition or the best condition available, then take good care of them. Keep records in their sleeves and stand albums on their sides. Joe prefers to play his old records on modern equipment, thus eliminating some of the scratchiness and hissing. However, the purist generally prefers to use phonographs that date from the period of the recordings. Joe does enjoy listening to old records on wind-up phonographs.

New
Victor Records
April 1923

"HIS MASTER'S VOICE"
REG. U.S. PAT. OFF.

ENRICO CARUSO
From a photograph taken at Sorrento, Italy
a few days before the great tenor's death

Victor Records, *with Caruso on the cover, April 1923,* **$20-25.**

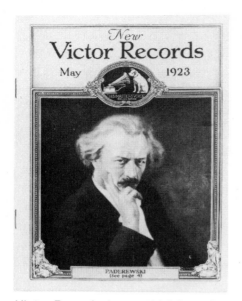

Victor Records *(a monthly) featuring Paderewski on the cover, May 1923,* **$20-25.**

Victor Records, *with John McCormack on the cover, December 1924,* **$20-25.**

Victor Records, *featuring Heifetz on the cover, January 1925,* **$15-20.**

An ad for the Victor-Victrola, **$5-7.**

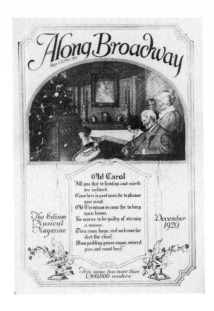

The Edison Musical Magazine, *published monthly, December 1920,* **$15-20.**

With the thousands of 78 RPMs and early LPs in Joe's collection, you might think that he would not have one favorite artist or recording, but he does. Bing Crosby is his all-time favorite male vocalist. And Bing's rendition of "Stardust," introduced on the Brunswick label in 1931, tops Joe's list. In mint condition, this record is worth approximately $75. Joe purchased a set of twelve Bing Crosby LPs on the Decca label, titled "Bing's Hollywood," for $500 just a few years ago. Recently he turned down an offer of more than $1,200 for this set.

There is a developing market for early LPs. Those with good market values were recorded by such artists as Nelson Eddy, Fred Astaire, Al Jolson, Kate Smith, Eddie Cantor, Judy Garland, Peggy Lee, and Frank Sinatra. *(Note: for the most part, 78s are obtained in the range of 50¢ to $5.)*

Records

Andrews Sisters, "Boogie Woogie Bugle Boy," Decca 3598, January 2, 1941, **$3.50-5.**

Armstrong, Louis (with his various groups), "My Heart," Okeh 8320, November 12, 1925, **$35-40.**

Armstrong, Louis (with his group), "Heebie Jeebies," Okeh 8300, February 26, 1926, **$35-40.**

Armstrong, Louis, "You Made Me Love You," Okeh 9447, November 17, 1926, **$25-30.**

Armstrong, Louis, "I Ain't Got Nobody," Okeh 8756, December 10, 1929, **$10-15.**

Astaire, Fred, "Cheek to Cheek," Brunswick 7486, June 26, 1935, **$4-5.**

Astaire, Fred, "Top Hat, White Tie and Tails," Brunswick 7487, June 27, 1935, **$4-5.**

Astaire, Fred (with Benny Goodman), "Who Cares," Columbia 35517, May 9, 1940, **$5-8.**

Bailey, Mildred, (Dorsey Brothers), "Lazy Bones," Brunswick 6587, June 6, 1933, **$5-7.**

Barnet, Charlies, and his orchestra, "Cherokee" (theme), Blue Bird 10373, July 17, 1939, **$3-5.**

Basie, Count, and his orchestra, "One O'Clock Jum" (theme), Decca 1363, July 7, 1937, **$8-10.**

Bernie, Ben, and his orchestra, "If You Knew Susie," Vocalion 15037, May 19, 1925, **$3-4.**

Blake, Eubie, "Sweet Lady" (piano solo), Emerson 10450, September 1921, **$15-20.**

Boswell Sisters, (Dorsey Brothers), "When I Take My Sugar To Tea," Brunswick 6083, March 19, 1931, **$5-7.50.**

Boswell, Connie, (with Crosby and Cantor), "Alexander's Ragtime Band," Decca 1887, January 26, 1938, **$6-8.**

Calloway, Cab, "Minnie the Moocher" (theme), Brunswick 6074, March 3, 1931, **$5-7.**

Calloway, Cab, "Hi-De-Ho Man," Columbia 37312, February 3, 1947, **$3-4.**

Carmichael, Hoagy, "Stardust," Gennett 6474, May 2, 1928, **$10-15.**

Casa Loma Orchestra, "Casa Loma Stomp," Okeh 41492, December 6, 1930, **$7-10.**

Clinton, Larry, and his orchestra, (Charlie Spevak), "Midnight in the Madhouse," Victor 25697, October 15, 1937, **$3-4.**

Cole, Nat "King," "Sweet Lorraine," Decca 9520, December 6, 1940, **$4-5.**

Cole, Nat "King," "Route 66," Capitol 256, March 15, 1946, **$3-5.**

Columbo, Russ, "Sweet and Lovely," Victor 22802, September 9, 1931, **$5-7.**

Columbo, Russ, "Prisoner of Love," Victor 22867, October 9, 1931, **$5-7.**

Crosby, Bing (with Al Rinker and Harry Barris-P. Whiteman), "I've Got the Girl," Columbia 924D, October 18, 1926, **$40-50.**

Crosby, Bing, "Where the Blue of the Night Meets the Gold of the Day," Brunswick 6226, November 23, 1931, **$20-25.**

Crosby, Bing (with Duke Ellington), "St. Louis Blues," 12″, Brunswick 20105, February 11, 1932, **$15-20.**

Crosby, Bing, "Brother, Can You Spare a Dime?," Brunswick 6414, October 25, 1932, **$8-10.**

Crosby, Bing, "Love In Bloom," Brunswick 6936, July 5, 1934, **$8-10.**

Crosby, Bob, and his orchestra (Bob Cats), "Big Noise from Winnetka," Decca 2208, October 14, 1938, **$4-6.**

Dorsey, Jimmy (Bing Crosby, Louis Armstrong, Frances Langford), "Pennies from Heaven Medley," 12″, Decca 15027, August 17, 1936, **$5-7.**

Dorsey, Tommy, "I'm Getting Sentimental Over You" (theme), Victor 25236, October 18, 1935, **$4-5.**

Dorsey, Tommy (Frank Sinatra), "Without a Song," 12″, Victor 36396, January 20, 1941, **$5-7.**

Garland, Judy, "You Made Me Love You" ("Dear Mr. Gable"), Decca 1463, September 24, 1937, **$5-7.**

Goodman, Benny, "Let's Dance" (theme), Columbia 35301, October 24, 1939, **$5-7.**

Pamphlet for Bing Crosby, issued as a promotion by Brunswick, **$20-25.**

Goodman, Benny (Peggy Lee), "Why Don't You Do Right?," Columbia 36652, July 27, 1942, **$5-7.**

Holiday, Billie, "The Man I Love," Vocalion 5377, December 13, 1939, **$5-7.**

Holiday, Billie, "Solitude," Decca 23853, February 13, 1947, **$5-7.**

Ink Spots, "If I Didn't Care," Decca 2286, January 12, 1939, **$3-4.**

James, Harry (Frank Sinatra), "All or Nothing at All," Columbia 35587, August 31, 1939, **$5-7.**

James, Harry (Frank Sinatra), "Ciribiribin," Columbia 35316, November 8, 1939, **$5-7.**

Jolson, Al, "That Haunting Melody," Victor 17037, December 22, 1911, **$30-35.**

Jolson, Al, "Avalon," Columbia A-2995, August 16, 1920, **$10-12.**

Song and Music, *with Dorothy Lamour on the cover, July 1941,* **$15-20.**

Rare records include those 78 RPMs that have photo labels showing the recording star, such as Bing Crosby, from his Paramount Picture Double or Nothing, *on the Brunswick label,* **$75-100.**

On the Brunswick label, Fred Astaire singing "Change Partners," from Carefree, **$75-100.**

Program from the Copacabana, showing all the stars who entertained there.

Program from Copacabana, starring the late, great Bobby Darin, **$8-10.**

A 45 EP (extended play) by Al Jolson. The early EPs and LPs are highly collectible, and prices are increasing almost daily. **$25-35.**

Metronome, *February 1945,* **$10-15.**

Sing It, *with Vincent Lopez and Frances Langford on the cover, 1935,* **$20-25.**

Brunswick Records promotion featuring Duke Ellington, **$20–25.**

Cue Magazine, *March 5, 1953, with Rosemary Clooney on the cover,* **$3-5.**

Jolson, Al, "There's a Rainbow Round My Shoulder," Brunswick 4033, August 20, 1928, **$12-15.**

Lombardo, Guy, "Cotton Picker's Ball," Gennett 5417, March 10, 1924, **$15-20.**

Lombardo, Guy (Kate Smith), "Too Late," Columbia 3578D, December 8, 1931, **$5-7.**

Lombardo, Guy (Al Jolson), "April Showers," Brunswick 6502, December 20, 1932, **$10-12.**

Martin, Mary (Eddie Duchin Orchestra), "My Heart Belongs to Daddy," Brunswick, 8282, November 30, 1938, **$5-6.**

Mills Brothers, "Tiger Rag," Brunswick 6197, October 21, 1931, **$8-10.**

Morgan, Helen, "Bill," Victor 21238, February 14, 1938, **$4-5.**

New Orleans Rhythm Kings, "Discontented Blues," Gennett 4967, August 29, 1922, **$50-60.**

Oliver, King, "Canal Street Blues," Gennett 5133, April 6, 1923, **$150-175.**

Oliver, King, "High Society Rag," Okeh 4933, June 22, 1923, **$150-175.**

Prima, Louis, "Chinatown, My Chinatown," Brunswick 7456, May 17, 1935, **$4-5.**

Rey, Alvino, "Nighty-Night" (theme), Bluebird 11041, February 3, 1941, **$3-4.**

Movie posters

All the posters listed are from Joe Franklin's collection. All are in mint condition. Abbreviations:

A=One sheet, 27" × 41"
B=22" × 28"
C=14" × 36"
WC=Window card

Abdul the Damned, Nils Asther, 1935, A, **$50-60.**

Accused, The, Loretta Young, 1948, A, **$25-45.**

Accused, The, Dolores Del Rio, 1936, A, **$100-125.**

Action in Arabia, George Sanders, 1944, A, **$35-50.**

Adventure In Manhattan, Jean Arthur, 1935, A, **$125-150.**

Adventure Island, Rhonda Fleming, 1947, A, **$25-35.**

Affair in Trinidad, Rita Hayworth, 1952, A, **$125-150.**

Angels of Broadway, Rita Hayworth, 1940, A, **$150-175.**

Anybody's Woman, Ruth Chatterton, 1930, A, **$150-175.**

Appointment in Honduras, Ann Sheridan, 1953, A, **$45-55.**

Arise, My Love, Claudette Colbert, 1940, A, **$75-100.**

Babes on Broadway, Judy Garland, A, **$450-550.**

Backstage, Anna Naegle, 1937, **$125-150.**

Balalaika, Nelson Eddy, 1939, A, **$100-125.**

Barkleys of Broadway, Ginger Rogers/Fred Astaire, 1948, A, **$50-75.**

Bathing Beauty, Esther Williams, 1944, A, **$100-125.**

Bedelia, Margaret Lockwood, 1947, A, **$25-35.**

Belle Star, Gene Tierney, 1941, A, **$125-150.**

Big Town Girl, Claire Trévor, 1938, A, **$100-125.**

Blackwell's Island, John Garfield, 1939, A, **$75-100.**

Poster for The Kid from Spain, *starring Eddie Cantor,* **$25-35.**

Blazing Saddles, Mel Brooks, A, **$10-15.**
Blonde Fever, Gloria Graham, 1944, A, **$25-35.**
Blue Dahlia, Alan Ladd and Veronica Lake, 1946, A, **$250-300.**
Brazil, Virginia Bruce, 1944, A, **$50-60.**
Broadway Musketeers, Ann Sheridan, 1938, A, **$100-125.**

Poster for The Sheik, *starring Rudolph Valentino,* **$20-25.**

Buck Rogers, Gil Gerard, 1980, A, **$10-15.**
Gilda, Rita Hayworth, B, **$150-175.**
Girl from Ave. A, Jane Withers, 1940, A, **$15-20.**
Harvey Girls, Judy Garland, 1945, A, **$200-250.**
Her Jungle Love, Dorothy Lamour, 1938, B, **$20-25.**
Home in Indiana, Jeanne Crain, 1944, A, **$15-20.**
Hush, Hush Sweet Charlotte, Bette Davis, C, **$10-15.**
Imitation of Life, Claudette Colbert, 1945, B, **$15-20.**
It's a Date, Deanna Durbin, 1940, **$250-300.**
Lulu Belle, Dorothy Lamour, 1948, A, **$50-60.**
Million Dollar Mermaid, Esther Williams, C, **$15-20.**
One Touch of Venus, Ava Gardner, 1948, A, **$40-50.**
Perils of Pauline, Betty Hutton, 1947, **$25-35.**
Prince and the Pauper, Errol Flynn, 1937, A, **$200-225.**
Sally, Irene and Mary, Alice Faye, 1938, WC, **$25-35.**
Sinbad the Sailor, Douglas Fairbanks, Jr., 1947, A, **$50-60.**

Song of the Open Road, Jane Powell, 1944, B, **$15-20.**
Tarzan Finds a Son, Johnny Weismuller, 1939, A, **$250-300.**
They All Kissed the Bride, Joan Crawford, A, **$25-35.**
Time Out for Rhythm, Ann Miller, A, **$50-75.**
Two-Faced Woman, Greta Garbo, 1941, A, **$225-250.**

Magazines

The variety of magazines dealing with all facets of show business is enormous. Listed are samples of the most available publications. The names following the dates are the celebrities who appeared on that issue's cover.

Movie Stars parade, *featuring the original blonde bombshell, Miss Betty Hutton, February 1944,* **$20-25.**

Stage Pictorial, *spring, 1945, featuring* On The Town, The Glass Menagerie, *and* Carousel, **$20-25.**

From Radio Round-Ups, *page 79.*

From 1932 Radio Round-Ups, **$20-25.**

PHOTOPLAY STUDIES

A MAGAZINE DEVOTED TO PHOTOPLAY APPRECIATION

Copyright, 1939, by Educational and Recreational Guides, Inc.

VOLUME VI	SERIES OF 1940	NUMBER 4

SHIRLEY TEMPLE AND JOHNNY RUSSELL IN "THE BLUE BIRD"

**RECOMMENDED BY THE MOTION-PICTURE COMMITTEE OF THE
DEPARTMENT OF SECONDARY TEACHERS OF THE
NATIONAL EDUCATION ASSOCIATION**

Photoplay Studies, *1940, Shirley Temple and Johnny Russell in* The Blue Bird, **$50-75.**

Photoplay
March 1925, Bessie Love, **$25-35.**
February 1929, Estelle Taylor, **$25-35.**
December 1932, Janet Gaynor, **$40-50.**
September 1935, Ann Harding, **$35-45.**
September 1935, Katharine Hepburn, **$40-50.**

The 1931 Favorite Recipes of the Movie Stars, *one of many cookbooks written by famous personalities,* **$30-35.**

June 1944, Olivia de Havilland, **$20-25.**
August 1945, Dianna Lynn, **$10-15.**
January 1947, Greer Garson, **$10-15.**
November 1947, Gene Tierney, **$15-20.**
December 1947, June Haver, **$10-15.**
May 1948, June Allyson, **$15-20.**
September 1948, Alan Ladd, **$15-20.**
August 1949, Shirley Temple, **$25-35.**
March 1940, Jane Wyman and Jimmy Stewart, **$10-15.**
March 1951, Betty Hutton, **$10-15.**
October 1954, Janet Leigh and Tony Curtis, **$10-12.**
February 1957, Rock Hudson, **$5-10.**
December 1947, Elizabeth Taylor, **$10-12.**
July 1959, Elizabeth Taylor and Eddie Fisher, **$7-10.**
July 1962, Elizabeth Taylor and Richard Burton, **$10-12.**

Modern Screen
February 1933, Bette Davis, **$30-40.**
March 1942, Sonja Henie, **$20-25.**
August 1946, Gregory Peck, **$15-20.**
January 1949, June Allyson, **$10-12.**
April 1953, Doris Day, **$5-10.**
September 1956, Jane Russell, **$10-12.**
December 1957, Debbie Reynolds and Eddie Fisher, **$10-12.**
June 1969, Elizabeth Taylor and Richard Burton, **$5-7.**

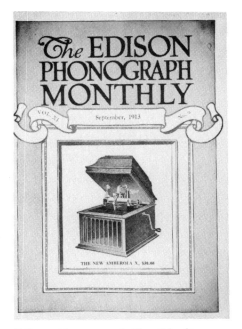

Laura La Plante, from Movie Star recipes.

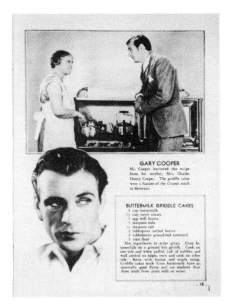

Gary Cooper and his mom, from Movie Star Recipes.

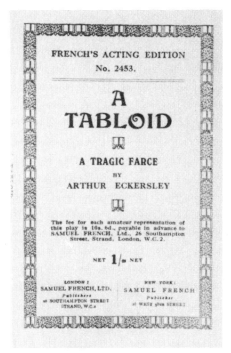

Edison Phonograph Monthly *for September 1913,* **$20-25.**

A 1914 tabloid with a play for acting schools. This edition featured "A Tragic Farce." **$3-5.**

Leisure Time, *December 13, 1953. On the cover, Mr. Tuesday Night, Mr. Television, Uncle Miltie (Milton Berle).* Leisure Time *contained the week's television schedule and articles.* **$15-20.**

100 LAUGHS TO EACH PAGE

Charles Chaplin's

Funny Sayings

Price
10 Cents

R. E. Sherwood
Publisher

19 John Street
New York City

Number One

KEEPS THE DOCTOR AWAY

Charlie Chaplin's Funny Sayings, *published in 1915. Among Joe's favorites are: "Very few men are smart enough to fill five reels with genuine daredevil acts of villainy and get away with coming out an angel at the end of the film." "A kiss is something like gossip—it goes from mouth to mouth." "Where love is only a dream, the marriage is an alarm clock."*

Imagine buying this copy of Who's Who in the Moving Pictures *for only ten cents in stamps back in 1915. On the cover, left to right, top to bottom: Hobart Bosworth, Francis X. Bushman, Anita Stewart, Crane Wilburn, Mary Pickford, Maurice Costello, Ben Wilson, Charles Chaplin, Edward Earle, Cissy Fitzgerald, Mary Leles Minter, and Theda Bara.*

Sheet Music Trade News, *June 1924,* **$20-25.**

Shirley Temple book, Little Playmates, *1936,* **$150-175.**

Tales of Manhattan

Around Town with Joe Doakes

STOOPNAGLE and BUD
CBS comics, on the new Procter & Gamble program

Information Department

DEAR JOE DOAKES:
I have three thousand shares of Star Flat at stock. What shall I do with it?
BILL SUCKER

DEAR BILL SUCKER:
I am sorry, but "Star Dust" is not through the mails and I cannot tell you what to do with Star Flat at stock. However, you can sell me off sometime as the paper company does not cover their messages.
Joe (Legal Advisor) Doakes

Idle Chatter Department

A coupla razzberries to Eddie Cantor for those 1890 jokes he has been pulling on the radio; also for stealing many gags from columns. The funny part of this program is that Eddie Cantor gets $6,000 for his hour every week. A few roses to Ward Wilson for his good mimicing. A razzberry to the boys who were so hard up that they had to book a gunman's moll and put her on display for the price of an admission. A few roses to Walter Winchell (the big stiff) for his good radio manner; we would give Walter a whole bunch of roses, but he spends too much time gagging that thar' Ben Bernie laddie, a whole ton of roses to my boss (I got a raise last month). That's enough of this tripe.

Nobody asked me, but if I were to select the 12 outstanding radio programs on the air I would pick these, and in order of their rating:

1. **Myrt and Marge (CBS)**—A human sketch presented wonderfully.
2. **Kate Smith (CBS)**—A good voice and choice of songs.
3. **Rudy Vallee (NBC)**—Because, after all, he is still Rudy Vallee.
4. **Boswell Sisters (CBS)**—Original and pleasing rhythm.
5. **Bing Crosby (CBS)**—Original and lively type of singing.
6. **Ben Bernie (NBC)**—For his humor even more than his fine music.
7. **Goldbergs (NBC)**—Any family will enjoy the Goldbergs.
8. **Morton Downey (CBS)**—A

Hello, everybody! Here is your Uncle Joe Doakes for his monthly chat and some of the latest gossip from the Main Stem of the world, Broadway. Before we go any further we just want to comment on the sale of "Star-Dust." We sold out last month, two weeks after we first appeared on the stands. A complete sell-out, and many fans had to do without their "Star-Dust" who tried to buy it late in the month. We are increasing our press run with this issue and hope we have another sell-out.

We always seem to get something on our good friend Ed Sullivan, who is doing so well on the Graphic. The biggest boner that Ed pulled last month was, "Society Girl will make a good movie if the leads are given to Eddie Robinson and Tallulah Bankhead or Eddie Robinson and James Cagney. (Just wait till that tough guy Cagney gets you Ed, he will tan your hide.)

RUDY VALLEE sure does a good job of murdering the Moo-Moo singing and gets a good laugh every time, as they all know how Rudy feels about those boys copping the "Flapper Play" away from him. Russ Columbo, by the way, is a big shot now and so is his manager Con Conrad. When they want to do anything or make a change in the program and the studio objects, they come back with "Well, it will be done my way or out I go." Won't it be fun if they are taken up on this sometime?

Screen Stories
July 1954, Caine Mutiny, **$10-15.**
December 1954, Elizabeth Taylor, **$10-12.**
January 1955, Frank Sinatra, **$10-15.**
February 1958, Doris Day, **$7-10.**
September 1959, Elizabeth Taylor, **$5-10.**
February 1963, Elizabeth Taylor, **$5-10.**
July 1968, Mia Farrow, **$5-10.**

Motion Picture
January 1944, Maureen O'Hara, **$15-20.**
August 1945, John Payne, **$15-20.**
February 1946, Gregory Peck, **$15-20.**

Twelve Best Radio Programs

ED. LOWRY
popular Master-of-Ceremonies, known from coast to coast, now playing at the Skouras Theatres (Academy and Audubon).

DORIS MAYE
Young and so fair!

Star Dust, *March 1932. Pages eight and nine list the twelve best radio programs of that time.* **$15-20.**

September 1946, Joan Leslie, **$10-15.**
June 1947, Jennifer Jones, **$15-20.**
March 1948, Susan Hayward, **$15-20.**
February 1949, Shirley Temple, **$20-230.**
July 1952, Ann Blyth, **$5-10.**
April 1955, June Allyson, **$5-10.**

Movie Life
May 1944, Ann Sheridan, **$15-25.**
December 1941, Abbott and Costello, **$25-35.**
August 1943, Clark Gable, **$25-35.**
1961 Movie Life Year Book, **$10-15.**

New York Amusements, *August 8, 1927, with Clara Bow on the cover,* **$5-8.**

New York Amusements, *July 2, 1928,* George White's Scandals, *with Ann Pennington on the cover,* **$3-5.**

New York Amusements, *February 20, 1928, with Leslie Howard on the cover,* **$5-7.**

New York Amusements, *June 25, 1919, with Judith Anderson on the cover,* **$3-5.**

From Stars of the Movies, *Tim McCoy, $50-75.*

Stars of the Movies, *featuring 250 portraits of the stars. This page shows Mary Astor.*

Really See
HOLLYWOOD

on a
FAWCETT
MOVIELAND TOUR

Two Great Tours this Year

Leaving Chicago
SATURDAY, JULY 15, 1939
SATURDAY, AUGUST 5, 1939

Sponsored by
FAWCETT PUBLICATIONS

Frank Sinatra, *a 1945 magazine,* **$50-75.**

Movieland Tours, 1939. Tour A was hosted by Allan Jones and Irene Harvey and included a cocktail party at Bel-Air Stables, owned jointly by Allen Jones and Robert Young. Tour B was hosted by Victor McLaughlin. **$5-6.**

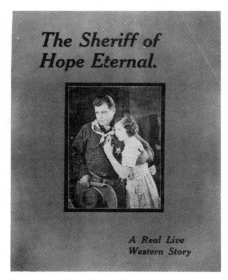

Book *for* The Sheriff of Hope Eternal, *a five-reel silent starring Jack Hoxie,* **$10-15.**

First National Good News, *May 15, 1928,* **$40-45.**

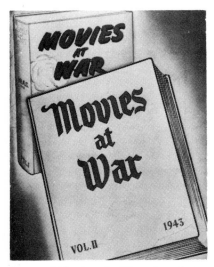

Copy *of* Movies At War, *dated 1943,* **$12-15.**

When a Man's a Man, *featuring western stars,* **$15-20.**

Hollywood, January 1940, Jane Withers, **$25-35.**
Hollywood, November 1942, John Payne, **$10-15.**
Large Photoplay, August 1938, Myrna Loy, **$25-35.**
Large Photoplay, March 1940, Olivia de Havilland, **$25-35.**
Movieland, April 1944, Ann Sheridan, **$15-20.**
Movieland, June 1946, June Allyson, **$5-10.**

The Hollywood Reporter *for the week of June 24, 1936,* **$20-25.**

Daily Review, *March 20, 1926. Gloria Swanson in* The Untamed Lady *on the cover.* **$25-30.**

The Monthly Screen Review *with Janet Gaynor on the cover, May 1929,* **$30-35.**

Movie Show, June 1947, Olivia de Havilland, **$12-15.**
Movie Show, July 1948, Loretta Young, **$8-10.**
Movie Spotlight, December 1954, Donna Reed, **$10-15.**
Movie Story, May 1948, Dana Andrews, **$5-10.**
Screenland, November 1939, Priscilla Lane, **$25-35.**
Screenland, February 1940, Barbara Stanwyck, **$25-30.**
Screenland, January 1951, Rita Hayworth, **$15-20.**
Silver Screen, November 1948, Tyrone Power and Gene Tierney, **$25-35.**

From the RKO Radio picture book for 1932-33, Bring 'Em Back Alive. *The annual picture book previewed upcoming movies. Sometimes the promoted films were never made, even though a script had been written and a cast chosen.*

RKO Radio picture book for 1932-1933. Preview books and announcement books were printed in limited quantities—sometimes not more than 250. They were distributed to only the best theaters. Because they are so rare, it is difficult to place a value on these items. Recently Joe Franklin was offered $3,000 for each of his announcement preview books. He turned down the offer!

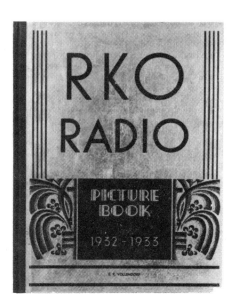

Playbill for Hello, Dolly, *starring Carol Channing, 1964,* **$2-3.**

You Said a Mouthful, *by Joe E. Brown, 1944. In this book, Joe E. Brown shares his experiences entertaining the troops.* **$20-25.**

Movie Song Sheets

A Certain Smile, 1958, Joan Fontaine, Rosano Brazzi, **$3-5.**
Barkleys of Broadway, The, 1946, Fred Astaire, Ginger Rogers, **$10-15.**
Bells of St. Mary's The, 1945, Bing Crosby, Ingrid Bergman, **$5-10.**
Buttons and Bows, 1948, Bob Hope, Jane Russell, **$5-10.**
Caddy, The, 1953, Martin and Lewis, **$5-8.**
College Rhythm, 1934, Joe Penner, Jack Oakie, **$5-10.**
Coney Island, 1942, Betty Grable, George Montgomery, Caeser Romero, **$10-15.**
Copacabana, 1947, Groucho Marx, Carmen Miranda, **$8-12.**
Dolly Sisters, 1945, Betty Grable, June Haver, **$10-20.**
Down Argentina Way, 1940, Betty Grable, George Montgomery, Carmen Miranda, **$15-20.**
Dynamite, 1929, Conrad Nagel, Kay Johnson, Charles Bickford, **$10-15.**
Forty Little Mothers, 1940, Eddie Cantor, **$10-20.**
Forty Second Street, 1932, Warner Baxter, Ruby Keeler, Bebe Daniels, Ginger Rogers, Dick Powell, **$5-10.**
Going My Way, 1944, Bing Crosby, **$5-8.**
Gold Diggers of 1933, 1933, Dick Powell, Joan Blondell, **$5-10.**
Golden Earrings, 1946, Ray Miland, Marlene Dietrich, **$3-5.**
Hello Frisco, Hello, 1943, Alice Faye, John Payne, **$10-15.**

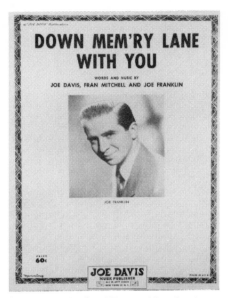

Sheet music for "Down Mem'ry Lane With You," with young Mr. Show Business on the cover.

Song Hits, *with Bing Crosby on the cover, November 1941,* **$10-15.**

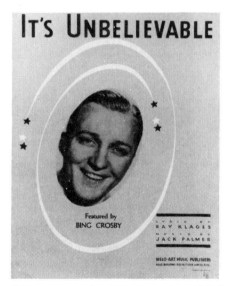

Sheet music for "It's Unbelieveable," with Crosby on the cover, 1935, **$10-15.**

Sheet music, "Swanee Shore," 1919 **$3-4.**

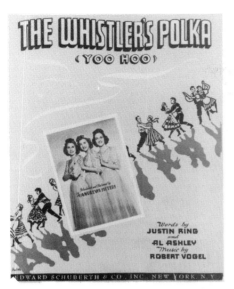

Sheet music, "The Whistler's Polka," the Andrews Sisters, **$4-5.**

Sheet music, "The Song in My Heart," Wayne King, **$3-4.**

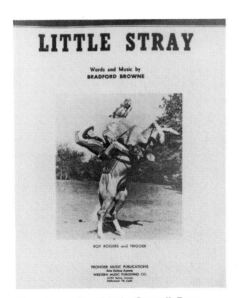

Sheet music, "Little Stray," Roy Rogers with Trigger, **$2-4.**

Sheet music, "The House that Jack Built for Jill," Bing Crosby and Frances Farmer on the cover, 1936, **$10-15.**

Sheet music, "Tom Thumb's Drum," Rudy Vallee on the cover, $3-4.

Sheet music for "Sunshine and Shadows" from the Ziegfeld Follies of 1920, $4-5.

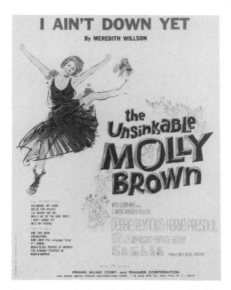

Sheet music for "I Ain't Down Yet" from The Unsinkable Molly Brown, starring Debbie Reynolds, 1961, $2-4.

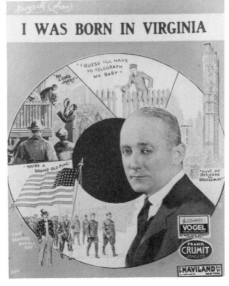

Sheet music, "I Was Born in Virginia," George M. Cohan on the cover, 1923, $10-15.

Sheet music for Glow-Worm
*(modern version by Johnny Mercer),
1952,* **$4-5.**

*Sheet music for "Praise the Lord
and Pass the Ammunition,"* **$3-4.**

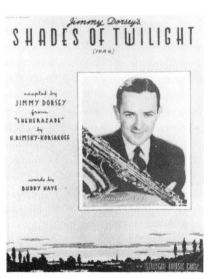

Sheet music featuring Jimmy Dorsey, "Shades of Twilight," **$3-5.**

*Sheet music featuring a photo of
Guy Lombardo, "Avalon Town,"* **$3-5.**

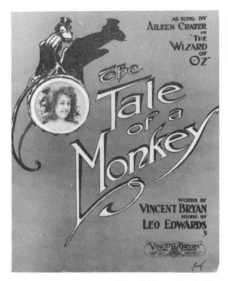

Sheet music from The Wizard of Oz,
1905. The song "Tale of a Monkey,"
$10-15.

Sheet music for The Little Millionaire, 1911, **$5-6.**

Here Come the Waves, 1944, Bing Crosby, Betty Hutton, **$5-10.**
High Noon, 1952, Gary Cooper, Grace Kelly, Katy Jurado, **$15-25.**
High Society Blues, 1937, Janet Gaynor, Charles Farrell, **$3-6.**
High, Wide and Handsome, 1937, Irene Dunne, Randolph Scott, **$5-10.**
Hoodlum, The, 1919, Mary Pickford, **$10-15.**
I Wonder Who's Kissing Her Now, 1946, June Haver, **$4-8.**
Iceland, 1942, Sonja Henie, John Payne, **$3-5.**
I'll Take Romance, 1937, Grace Moore, **$10-15.**
It Happened in Brooklyn, 1947, Frank Sinatra, Jimmy Durante, Peter Lawford,
    Kathryn Grayson, **$5-10.**
Joker Is Wild, The, 1957, Frank Sinatra, Jeanne Crain, Mitzie Gaynor, **$5-8.**
Laura, 1945, Gene Tierney, **$2-5.**
Lady in the Dark, 1943, Ginger Rogers, **$5-10.**
Las Vegas Nights, 1941, Tommy Dorsey, Phil Regan, **$1-5.**
Make a Wish, 1937, Bobby Breen, Basil Rathbone, Marion Claire, **$8-12.**
Mad About Musc, 1938, Deanna Durbin, **$5-10.**
Marianne, 1929, Marion Davies, **$5-10.**
Melody of Broadway, 1940, Fred Astaire, Eleanor Powell, **$15-20.**
Midnight Rounders, 1921, Eddie Cantor, **$5-10.**
Moulin Rouge, 1933, Constance Bennett, **$5-10.**
My Wild Irish Rose, 1947, Dennis Morgan, Arlene Dahl, **$5-7.**
One Hour with You, 1932, Maurice Chevalier, **$5-7.**
Operation 13, 1934, Gary Cooper, Marion Davies, **$15-20.**
Paleface, The, 1948, Bob Hope, Jane Russell, **$10-15.**
Passage to Marseille, 1944, Humphrey Bogart, **$15-20.**

Peg O' My Heart, 1933, Marion Davies, **$10-12.**

Possessed, 1942, Joan Crawford, Clark Gable, **$15-20.**

Ride 'Em Cowboy, 1941, Abbott and Costello, Dick Foran, **$8-12.**

Road to Morocco, 1942, Bob Hope, Bing Crosby, Dorothy Lamour, **$5-10.**

Roberta, 1933, Irene Dunne, Ginger Rogers, Fred Astaire, **$10-15.**

Rose of Washington Square, 1939, Tyrone Power, Al Jolson, Alice Faye, **$8-12.**

Say It with Songs, 1929, Al Jolson, **$10-15.**

Show Business, 1943, Eddie Cantor, Geeorge Montgomery, **$5-10.**

Singing Fool, 1929, Al Jolson, **$10-15.**

Street Angel, 1928, Janet Gaynor, Charles Farrell, **$3-6.**

Suzy, 1936, Jean Harlow, Franchot Tone, Cary Grant, **$25-30.**

Sweet Rosie O'Grady, 1943, Betty Grable, Robert Young, **$10-15.**

Swing Time, 1936, Fred Astaire, Ginger Rogers, **$10-15.**

Sweet and Low Down, 1944, Benny Goodman, Jack Oakie, Linda Darnell,
$5-10.

Tammy, 1957, Debbie Reynolds, **$1-5.**

Thank Your Luck Stars, 1943, Humphrey Bogart, Eddie Cantor, Bette Davis,
Erroll Flynn, **$10-15.**

There's No Business Like Show Business, 1954, Marilyn Monroe, Donald
O'Connor, Ethel Merman, **$15-20.**

Three Little Girls in Blue, 1946, June Haver, George Montgomery, Vivian Blaine,
Celeste Holm, **$4-8.**

Too Much Harmony, 1933, Bing Crosby, **$5-10.**

Top Speed, 1930, Joe E. Brown, **$10-15.**

When My Baby Smiles at Me, 1948, Betty Grable, Dan Dailey, **$10-15.**

White Christmas, 1953, Bing Crosby, Danny Kaye, Rosemary Clooney, Vera
Ellen, **$5-10.**

Words and Music, 1937, June Allyson, Judy Garland, Mickey Rooney, **$10-15.**

Lobby Cards

Lobby cards are one of Joe Franklin's passions. He believes that lobby cards
are still "sleepers" that will rise in value. Lobby cards came in sets of eight,
with seven scenes and one main title card featuring the full cast. Full sets
are more valuable than single cards. Joe suggests collecting cards that feature big-name stars, such as Joan Crawford, Bette Davis, John Garfield, and
Humphrey Bogart. But you should buy what is affordable and appealing to
you. Lobby cards, best kept in a frame under glass, make inexpensive and
handsome wall hangings.

Abbott and Costello, *Abbott and Costello Meet the Invisible Man,* 1951, complete set $100-125.

Astaire, Fred, *Roberta,* 1935, **$175-200**

Bacall, Lauren (Humphrey Bogart), *The Big Sleep,* 1946, **$250-300**

Bara, Theda, *The Devil's Daughter,* 1915 (black and white), **$50-75**

Belushi, John, *The Blues Brothers, 1980,* **$25-35.**

Berkeley, Busby, *Gold Diggers of 1935,* title card **$200-225**

Berle, Milton, *Over My Dead Body,* 1942, complete set **$75-100**

Lobby card, Women Are Like That, **$50-75.**

Lobby card, Strike Me Pink, *1936,* **$40-50.**

Lobby card, Boy Trouble, *Paramount, 1939,* **$35-45.**

Lobby card, Crime Ring, **$35-45.**

Lobby card, Flesh and Fantasy, *1943,* **$75-100.**

Lobby card, Deception, *1946,* **$75-100.**

Lobby card, Gold Diggers in Paris, *1938,* **$100-125.**

Lobby card, Buy Me That Town, *1941,* **$50-75.**

Lobby card, Serenade, *1956,* **$20-25.**

Bogart, Humphrey, *Sirocco,* 1951, complete set **$150-175**
Bogart, Humphrey, *Treasure of Sierra Madre,* 1948, **$125-150**
Bow, Clara, *It,* 1927, **$100-125**
Brooks, Mel, *Young Frankenstein,* 1974, complete set **$25-35**
Burns and Allen, *Love in Bloom,* 1935, **$45-50**
Cagney, James, *Great Guy,* 1936, **$100-110**
Cagney, James, *Yankee Doodle Dandy,* 1942, **$100-125**
Chan, Charlie (Warner Oland), *Charlie Chan at the Olympics,* 1937, **$100-125**
Chan, Charlie (Sidney Toler), *The Shanghai Cobra,* 1945, **$100-125**
Chaplin, Charlie, *A Dog's Life,* 1918 (black and white), **$300-350**
Chaplin, Charlie, *The Kid,* 1921 (sepia), title card **$700-750**
Clift, Montgomery (Elizabeth Taylor), *Suddenly Last Summer,* 1960, **$15-20**
Coogan, Jackie (*The Kid*—see Chaplin, Charlie)
Cooper, Gary, *High Noon,* 1952, **$35-45**
Cooper, Gary (Jean Arthur), *Mr. Deeds Goes to Town,* 1936, **$125-150**
Crawford, Joan, *Flamingo Road,* 1949 (duo-tone), complete set **$75-100**
Crawford, Joan, *The Gorgeous Hussy,* 1936, title card **$200-225**
Crosby, Bing, *A Connecticut Yankee,* 1949, complete set **$100-125**
Crosby, Bing, *She Loves Me Not,* 1934, **$50-75**
Crosby, Bing, *White Christmas,* 1954, complete set **$100-125**
Dean, James, *East of Eden,* 1955, **$50-75**
Dietrich, Marlene (Gary Cooper), *Desire,* 1936, **$225-250**

Dix, Richard, *Devil's Playground,* 1936, **$25-30**
Durante, Jimmy, *Carnival,* 1935, title card **$50-75**
Eastwood, Clint, *Play Misty for Me,* 1971, **$25-30**
Flynn, Errol (Olivia de Havilland), *Captain Blood,* 1935, **$600-650**
Flynn Errol, *They Died with Their Boots On,* 1941, **$125-150**
Fonda, Henry, *The Grapes of Wrath,* 1940, **$200-225**
Gable, Clark, *Call of the Wild,* 1935, **$150-175**
Gable, Clark, *Run Silent, Run Deep,* 1958, **$50-75**
Gable, Clark, *San Francisco,* 1936, **$225-250**
Garfield, John, *Nobody Lives Forever,* 1946, complete set **$100-125**
Gaynor, Janet, *State Fair,* 1933, title card **$125-150**
Gilbert, John, *Desert Nights,* 1929, **$50-75**
Heston, Charlton, *Beneath the Planet of the Apes, complete set* **$35-50**
Hope, Bob, *My Favorite Brunette,* 1947, complete set **$75-100**
Laurel and Hardy, *The Bohemian Girl,* 1936, **$275-300**
Lemmon, Jack, *Days of Wine and Roses,* 1963, **$25-30**
Lombard, Carole, *The Princess Comes Across,* 1936, **$50-65**
Lugosi, Bela, *The Return of Chandu,* 1934 (serial), title card, chapter four,
  $40-50
Marx Brothers, *A Night at the Opera,* 1935, **$300-325**
Mitchum, Robert, *Man in the Middle,* 1964, complete set **$20-25**
Monroe, Marilyn (Mickey Rooney), *The Fireball,* 1950, **$35-40**
Newman, Paul, *Hud,* 1963, **$10-15**
Navarro, Ramon, *The Night Is Young,* 1935, **$30-35**
Raft, George (Anna Mae Wong), *Limehouse Blues,* 1934, **$50-75**
Robinson, Edward G., *The Sea Wolf,* 1941, complete set **$250-275**
Sellers, Peter, *The Pink Panther,* 1964, **$10-15**
Sinatra, Frank, *Ocean's 11,* 1960, complete set **$50-60**
Stallone, Sylvester, *Rocky II,* 1979, complete set **$20-25**
Temple, Shirley, *Captain January,* 1936, **$200-225**
Weissmuller, Johnny (Maureen O. Sullivan), *Tarzan Finds a Son,* 1939, **$50-75**

Movie pressbooks

Theater books, also called pressbooks, are of moderate value today, but due to the increasing interest in these items, prices are expected to rise.

Pressbooks are sent to theater managers to aid in the promotion of a film. They include a synopsis of the film, biographies of the cast, illustrations of the prepared advertisements for the film, posters, lobby cards, and other visual promotional materials. The pressbook also contains information on publicity and promotion, and illustrations of various products and/or premiums associated with the film. Sometimes pressbooks are extra large, depending on the importance of the film. One Paramount pressbook used Harold Lloyd's name more than one thousand times!

Abbott and Costello Meet Captain Kidd, Warner Brothers, 1952, 12 pages, **$10-12.**

(Continued on page 161)

Program for Roman Scandals, *Gem Theater,* **$8-10.**

Lucky Devils, *starring Bill Boyd (but not in the role of Hopalong Cassidy),* **$5-6.**

Program from Liberty Theatre, Bernardsville, New Jersey. (Movie memorabilia from small-town theaters is becoming highly collectible.) **$2-4.**

A 1931 issue of the New York Times *which had an ad for the Brooklyn Paramount, where Eddie Cantor was appearing.*

A 1937 theater program for Ali Baba Goes to Town *with Eddie Cantor. Also playing was a full-length feature titled* Review of Walt Disney's Academy Award Winner *in technicolor. The Saturday matinee showed Episode Eight of Radio Patrol, the news, and a community sing.* **$10-15.**

Program from October 12, 1933. The theater is Grauman's Chinese, the motion picture Come Up And See Me Sometime, *the star Mae West. The photograph on the cover, which is a loose insert, was autographed by Mae West.* **$175-200.**

WALT DISNEY'S MICKEY MOUSE

Terrific exploitation backs every Mickey Mouse picture!

Nationally syndicated cartoon strips in the largest newspapers — articles in the best magazines — candy — toys — games — books and scores of other tie-ups! Last but not least there's the "Mickey Mouse Club", a vast alive organization of members whose great interest in Mickey brings them to your theatre every time he is on your screen!

The greatest cartoon character on the World's Screen. Everybody knows and loves him! His antics brighten the tiny tot and the tottering monarch! He has sold more tickets than all the epic pictures put together. He's in the newspapers, the high-brow magazines —and on the toy store shelf! You couldn't get away from Mickey if you wanted to—and Gosh! who'd make a mistake like that!

Mickey Mouse, from the Columbia Pictures announcement book, 1932-1933.

Abbott and Costello Meet the Keystone Cops, Universal, 1954, 8 pages, **$10-12.**

Ace Drummond, Universal Serial, 1936 (Filmcraft re-release), John King, Jean Rogers, Noah Berry, Jr., 8 pages, contains synopsis of all thirteen chapters. **$15-20.**

Across the Pacific, Warner Brothers, 1942, Humphrey Bogart, Mary Astor, Sydney Greenstreet, 24 pages, **$100-125.**

Adventures of Captain Africa, serial, Columbia, 1955, John Hart. 12 pages, complete synopsis of all fifteen chapters. **$25-30.**

Affair with a Stranger, RKO, 1953, Jean Simmons, Victor Mature, 16 pages, **$10-15.**

After Your Own Heart, Twentieth Century-Fox, 1921, Tom Mix, 8 pages, **$150-175.**

(Continued on page 165)

From the Columbia announcement book, 1932-1933, stars including Adolphe Menjou, Barbara Stanwyck, Charles Bickford, Buck Jones, and Tim McCoy.

Promotion for Cleopatra, *starring Claudette Colbert,* $15-20.

From the RKO Radio preview book, 1944-1945, Fibber McGee and Molly in
Heavenly Days.

From the RKO Radio preview book, 1944-1945, Cary Grant in None But the
Lonely Heart.

*From the RKO Radio preview book, 1944-1945, the promotional material for
Cary Grant in* The Greatest Gift. *The copy reads: "Wait'll you see what
Cary Grant does with this golden opportunity—one of the meatiest roles of
his career—the portrayal of a man who is granted his wish that he'd never
been born...and sees how things would have been without him. A
natural—and a knockout!" This movie was never made.*

From the RKO Radio preview book, 1944-1945, "Young Blue Eyes/The Voice,"
Mr. Frank Sinatra in American Carnival. *This movie was never made.*

REMEMBER THE "GOOD OLD DAYS"?

Joe Franklin

Well, they're coming back... Sept. 15, 1972 and Jan. 22, 1973

That's when Joe Franklin will personally take you on a nostalgic 8 day cruise into the past aboard the luxurious T.S.S. Queen Anna Maria to San Juan and St. Thomas and on a 12 day Caribbean and South American cruise on the elegant T.S.S. Olympia.

To make the past *really* come alive, Joe and Greek Line have planned a full schedule of special activities. You'll be entertained by old time favorites appearing in person. See the following silent classics: *Tarzan of the Apes* with Elmo Lincoln; *The Drop Kick*, starring Richard Barthelmess; and *Tillie's Punctured Romance*, featuring the incomparable Charlie Chaplin and Marie Dressler, *Teddy at the Throttle* with Wallace Beery and Gloria Swanson. The movies will be introduced by Joe, who will entertain and amuse you with anecdotes about the stars.

In the evenings, you'll want to watch vintage early talkies. Among the outstanding movies we have selected for you are: a series of early sound musicals starring Jimmy Durante, Kate Smith, Rudy Vallee, Joe E. Brown, Ted Lewis, George M. Cohan and many others.

In addition, you'll view rarely seen reels of short subjects from Joe Franklin's private library. They feature Fatty Arbuckle, Buster Keaton, W. C. Fields, Harry Langdon, Bob Hope, Harold Lloyd, Jack Benny, Bing Crosby, and other top comedians.

Highlights of our cruises will be special nights devoted to honoring superstars of the past. One evening will feature Humphrey Bogart, another Tyrone Power, and a third, Maurice Chevalier. Also, there will be Greta Garbo, Eddie Cantor and Al Jolson Festivals, and a series of old-time newsreel nights will be highlighted.

Other exciting events are a Period Costume Ball, lavish Jim Brady Dinner, memorabilia exhibit and sing-alongs. Plus many other activities to surprise and delight you.

A promotional piece highlighting the activities from one of Joe's Memory Lane Cruises. The twelve days in the Caribbean include such events as a period costume ball, memorabilia exhibits, evenings with vintage early talkies and early sound musicals, as well as silent classics.

The Little American, *starring Mary Pickford,* **$30-40.**

All Ashore, Columbia, 1953, Mickey Rooney, 16 pages, **$10-12.**
Always Leave Them Laughing, Warner Brothers, 1949, Milton Berle, Virginia Mayo, 16 pages, **$15-20.**
Anything Goes, Paramount, 1956, Bing Crosby, 24 pages, **$25-35.**
Auntie Mame, Warner Brothers, 1958, Rosalind Russell, 16 pages with advertising supplement, **$15-20.**
Between Two Worlds, Warner Brothers, 1944, John Garfield, 16 pages with advertising supplement, color covers, **$35-40.**

(Continued on page 183)

Pressbook for The Big Broadcast, Paramount, *1938.*

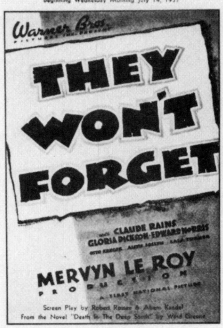

Cast of Characters

Andy Griffin	Claude Rains	Detective Pindar	Granville Bates
Sybil Hale	Gloria Dickson	Mrs. Mountford	
Robert Hale	Edward Norris		Ann Shoemaker
Gleason	Otto Kruger	Governor Mountford	
Bill Brock	Allyn Joslyn		Paul Everton
Mary Clay	Lana Turner	Harmon	Donald Briggs
Imogene Mayfield	Linda Perry	Mrs. Clay	Sybil Harris
Joe Turner	Elisha Cook, Jr.	Shattuck Clay	Trevor Bardette
Detective Laneart	Cy Kendall	Luther Clay	Elliott Sullivan
Tump Redwine		Ransom Clay	Wilmer Hines
	Clinton Rosemond	Drugstore Clerk	Eddie Acuff
Carlisle P. Buxton		Reporter	Frank Faylen
	E. Alyn Warren	Judge Moore	Leonard Mudie
Mrs Hale	Elizabeth Risdon	Confederate	Harry Davenport
Jim Timberlake	Clifford Soubier	Soldiers	Harry Beresford
			Edward McWade

VITAPHONE FEATURETTES

"PICTORIAL REVUE #12"

"PLENTY OF MONEY AND YOU"
A "Merrie Melody" Cartoon in Technicolor

STRAND NEWS EVENTS

PROGRAM SUBJECT TO CHANGE WITHOUT NOTICE

Program from The Strand in new York City, featuring Mae Murray in The Plow Girl, **$10-15.**

Program for the Strand Theatre, July 14, 1937, **$5-7.**

This material was used by the major studios to introduce up-and-coming stars. **$40-50.**

Do any of these new faces look familiar?

More new faces from M-G-M.

This is the last group of new faces. Some of these young actors and actresses became famous performers who entertained on the big screen as well as on early TV.

Paramount Pictures announcement book, 1930-1931, at least **$3,000.**

From the Paramount Pictures announcement book, 1930-1931, Kid Boots
with Jack Oakie. Eddie Cantor starred in Kid Boots *on Broadway and in
the silent film, which was released October 31, 1926. This sound version
was abandoned and the movie was never made.*

From the Paramount Pictures announcement book, 1930-1931, Harold Lloyd in Feet First.

From the Paramount Pictures announcement book, 1930-1931, the Marx Brothers in Animal Crackers.

A 1978 program from On Stage at Radio City Music Hall, starring Old Blue Eyes, Mr. Frank Sinatra, **$5-7.**

The Stolen J-O-O-L-S, *which featured a cast of fifty-five stars,* **$20-25.**

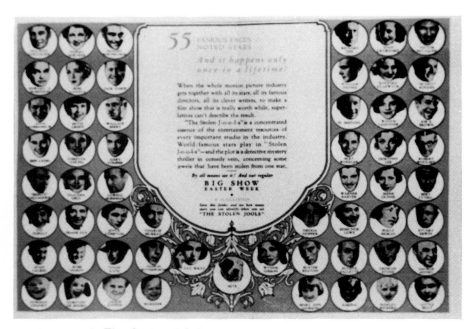

All the stars in The Stolen J-O-O-L-S.

The interior of the preview shows fifty-two pictures, including eight westerns and eight melodramas. Among the films listed are some of Joe's favorite "B" movies, including Conrad Nagel in Yellow Cargo and Tex Ritter in the Range Rider series.

Program for Cornelia Otis Skinner at the Shubert Theatre in New York City, **$2-4.**

Program for the Lyric Theatre, 1906, **$5-7.**

From United Artists, Walt Disney's 1936 Silly Symphonies *announcement book. Disney material is highly collectible.*

From United Artists, Eddie Cantor in Strike Me Pink, *announcement book, 1936.*

From United Artists, Charlie Chaplin *in* Modern Times, *announcement book, 1936.*

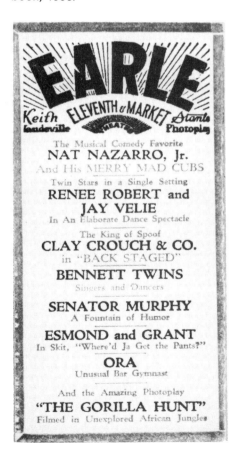

Promotion for Ben's Kid, *a Diamond S (Selig) production, July 1, 1909, $10-12.*

Program from the Earle (Keith Vaudeville Circuit), $5-8.

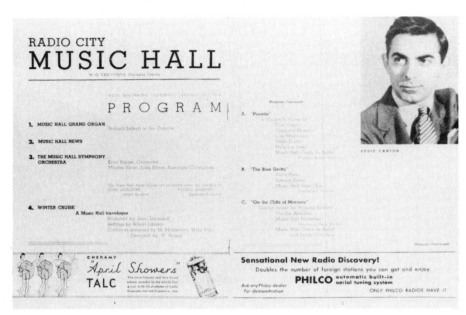

Program from Radio City Music Hall, January 16, 1936, **$20-25.**

Early sound films festival at the Fifth Avenue Cinema, 1954, **$4-5.**

Monogram Pictures Pressbook for Road to Happiness, starring John Boles, **$20-25.**

Program from the Palace Theatre, New York City, **$10-15.**

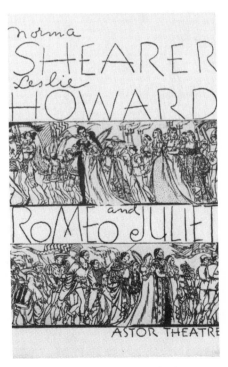

Program for Romeo and Juliet, *starring Norma Shearer and Leslie Howard, 1937,* **$5-7.**

Program for Roman Scandals *showing how the program made use of lobby cards to promote other features on the monthly bill.*

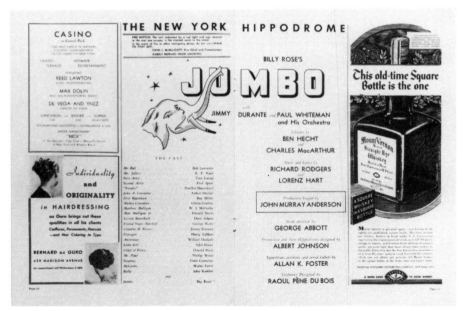

The cast from the program for Billy Rose's Jumbo. *Entire program,* **$25-35.**

The inside of the M-G-M booklet shows the bands in the M-G-M movies:
Louis Armstrong (Trumpet King of Swing) in Cabin in the Sky; Bob Crosby
in Presenting Lily Mars (starring Judy Garland); Jimmy Dorsey in I Dood It,
starring Red Skelton; Tommy Dorsey (the Sentimental Gentleman of Swing)
in DuBarry Was a Lady, starring Lucille Ball and Red Skelton; Duke Ellington in Cabin in the Sky; Gene Krupa (the ace drummer man) in Girl Crazy
and Anchors Aweigh; Kay Kaiser (the Ol' Professor); Harry James, Dick Jur-
gens, and Vaughn Monroe.

From M-G-M, a promo showing Leo
the Lion as a bandleader.

Program for Showboat (Movietone),
starring Laura La Plante, **$15-20.**

Program for Maud Muller, *a silent film from Essanay Films,* **$5-8.**

Chicago Stagebill *for* Hold Onto Your Hats *at the Grand Opera House, starring Al Jolson, Martha Raye, and Jack Whiting, July 15, 1940,* **$10-15.**

Program from the Roxy Theatre in New York City, February 21, 1931. The motion picture was Dracula, with Bela Lugosi and Helen Chandler. **$25-35.**

Loew's Weekly, *a theatre program, April 18, 1940,* **$10-12.**

Program for Alexander's Rag Time Band, *starring Tyrone Power and Alice Faye, February 2, 1938, The Roxy Theatre in New York City.* **$20-25.**

Promotional pamphlet for Lux toilet soap, featuring Barbara Stanwyck on the cover, **$4-5.**

Preview from Grand National Pictures, 1936-1937, **$30-40.**

Program for Gold Diggers of Broadway *(Vitaphone), the Winter Garden Theatre, New York City,* **$15-20.**

Paramount promotion, $15-20.

Page two from the Paramount Theatre Inaugural showing the architect's drawing of the Paramount building and theatre.

Paramount Progress, *July 13, 1916,* $10-12.

The George M. Cohan Theatre.

The Great Ziegfeld, *February 27, 1937* (Picturegoers Supplement), **$20-25.**

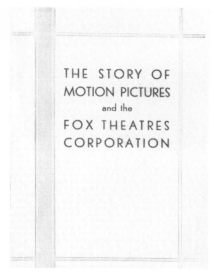

The Story of Motion Pictures, *published by Fox, 1932,* **$20-25.**

B. F. Keith's Vaudeville program, *June 25, 1925,* **$10-12.**

Billie Burke in *Peggy,* **$5-8.**

RKO Newsette, *February 23, 1935, featuring* Wings in the Dark, *starring Myrna Loy,* **$8-10.**

The program from Lafayette Square Opera House, Washington, D.C., Sunday, January 22, 1899, for John Philip Sousa and his band. **$45-55.**

Program for the 1941 Hollywood Ice Production's tour, starring Sonja Henie, **$8-10.**

From the George M. Cohan Theatre, a program for Two Little Girls in Blue, *August 15, 1921,* **$15-20.**

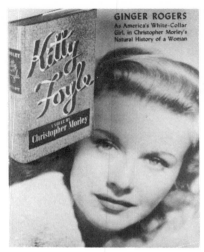

From the RKO Pictures announcement book, 1940-1941, Ginger Rogers in Kitty Foyle. *The novel shown is a pop-up. Pop-ups enhanced the visual effects of the announcement books.*

From the RKO Pictures announcement book, 1940-1941, Jean Arthur in The Devil and Miss Jones.

Big Knife, The, United Artists, 1955, Jack Palance, Ida Lupino, 20 pages with herald, **$20-25.**

Black Arrow, Columbia, serial, 1944, Robert Scott, Adele Jergens, 12 pages with complete synopsis of all fifteen chapters, **$40-50.**

Blazing Guns, Monogram Pictures, 1943, Ken Maynard, Hoot Gibson, 8 pages **$25-35.**

Blood Alley, Warner Brothers, 1955, John Wayne, 20 pages, **$20-25.**

Blue Bird, The, Twentieth Century-Fox, 1940, Shirley Temple, 20 pages with advertising supplement, color front cover, posters illustrated in full color, **$200-275.**

Cattle Queen of Montana, RKO, 1954, Ronald Reagan, Barbara Stanwyck, 12 pages, **$15-20.**

Charlie McCarthy Viataphone Shorts, Warner Brothers, 1937, Edgar Bergen, Charlie McCarthy. Six-page pressbook is for six different shorts, **$40-50.**

Checkers, Twentieth Century-Fox, Jane Withers, 8 pages, **$20-25.**

Dynamite Canyon, Monogram Pictures, 1941, Tom Keene, 8 pages, **$15-20.**

Flying Leathernecks, RKO, 1951, John Wayne, 16 pages with color front cover, **$30-35.**

G-Men, Warner Brothers, 1935, James Cagney, 20 pages with advertising supplement, **$250-275.**

George White's Scandals, Twentieth Century-Fox, 1934, Rudy Vallee, Jimmy Durante, Alice Faye. Measures 15¾" × 21¾", 16 pages with advertising supplement, **$200-250.**

Program cover for the world premiere of Jack London's The Sea Wolf, *starring Edward G. Robinson, Ida Lupino, and John Garfield. The premiere of this motion picture was aboard the luxury liner S.S. America. It was the first time a premiere was held on board a ship.*

A photograph showing all the stars who attended the premiere of The Sea Wolf. *Left to right, top to bottom: Julie Bishop, Morris Wrixon, Alexis Smith, Charles Ruggles, Maria Montez, John Garfield, Marguerite Chapman, Kay Aldridge, Jean Ames, Alice Talton, Georgia Carroll, Joan Perry, Hobart Bosworth, Mary Astor, Edward Robinson, Priscilla Lane, and Ronald Reagan. Value for the complete set of log, program, and photograph,* **$250-350.**

Godfather, The, Paramount, 1972, Marlon Brando, Al Pacino, James Caan, Robert Duvall, 6 pages, **$15-20.**

Guys and Dolls, Metro-Goldwyn-Mayer, 1955, Marlon Brando, Frank Sinatra, Jean Simmons, Vivian Blaine. Giant five-section pressbook with 110 pages, color herald, publicity supplement, one color portfolio with ties and posters in color, **$125-150.**

Hard Day's Night, United Artists, 1964, The Beatles, 12 pages, **$20-25.**

Hollywood Round-Up, Columbia, 1937, Buck Jones, Helen Twelvetrees, **$75-100.**

Is Everybody Happy, Columbia, 1943, Ted Lewis and his orchestra, 16 pages, **$10-15.**

Kentucky Moonshine, Twentieth Century-Fox, 1938, the Ritz Brothers, Tony Martin, 16″ × 21½″, 16 pages, **$45-50.**

Key Largo, Warner Brothers, 1948, Humphrey Bogart, Lauren Bacall, Edward G. Robinson, Lionel Barrymore, Claire Trevor, Thomas Gomez, 12 pages with advertising supplement, **$175-200.**

Lady Killer, Warner Brothers, 1933, James Cagney, Mae Clark, 26 pages, **$125-150.**

Last Bandit, The, Republic Pictures, 1949, Wild Bill Elliott, 4 pages, **$10-15.**

Law of the Texan, Columbia, 1935, Buck Jones, 8 pages, **$75-100.**

Lawless Riders, Columbia, 1935, Ken Maynard, 8 pages, **$75-100.**

Little Miss Marker, Paramount, 1934, Shirley Temple, 20 pages, **$400-500.**

Manhattan, United Artists, 1979, Woody Allen, 16 pages, **$10-12.**

On Your Toes, Warner Brothers, 1939, Zorina, 16 pages with advertising supplement, **$35-45.**

Once Upon a Time, Columbia, 1944, Cary Grant, Betsy Blair, 20 pages, **$35-45.**

Raven, The, American International, 1963, Vincent Price, Peter Lorre, Boris Karloff, Jack Nicholson, 16 pages, **$30-35.**

Riding Wild, Columbia, 1934, Tim McCoy, 8 pages, **$75-100.**

Serpico, Paramount, 1973, Al Pacino, 6 pages with advertising supplement, **$5-10.**

Spy Who Loved Me, The, United Artists, 1977, Roger Moore, 12 pages, **$10-12.**

Streetcar Named Desire, A, Warner Brothers, 1951, Marlon Brando, Vivien Leigh, 29 pages with advertising supplement, **$10-15.**

T-Men, Eagle-Lion, 1947, Dennis O'Keefe, 32 pages with color covers, **$15-20.**

Tarzan's Desert Mystery, RKO, 1943, Johnny Weissmuller, 12 pages, **$35-45.**

3-Ring Circus, Paramount, 1954, Martin and Lewis, 24 pages, **$20-25.**

Thunder River Feud, Monogram Pictures, 1942 Ray "Crash" Corrigan, John "Dusty" King, Max "Alibi" Terhune as "The Range Busters." 8 pages, **$25-35.**

Treasure of the Sierra Madre, The, Warner Brothers, 1948, Humphrey Bogart, Walter Huston, Tim Holt, Bruce Bennett, 16 pages with advertising supplement, **$125-150.**

Utah Trail, Grand National, Tex Ritter, 8 pages, **$30-35.**

Wyoming Renegades, Columbia, 1954, Phil Carey, 8 pages, **$8-10.**

Yankee Doodle Dandy, Warner Brothers, 1942, James Cagney, 36 pages with advertising supplement, **$150-175.**

Zero Hour, Paramount, 1957, Dana Andrews, Linda Darnell, 12 pages, **$7-10.**

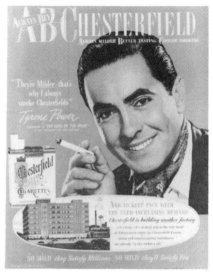

An ad for Chesterfield cigarettes, featuring Tyrone Power, **$20-25.**

A 1952 ad for Pabst Blue Ribbon beer with Eddie Cantor, **$20-25.**

An ad for Pabst Blue Ribbon beer, featuring Eddie Cantor. Ads with personalities are becoming highly collectible. **$20-25.**

Postcard featuring Ella Fitzgerald as she appeared at an engagement at Basic Street East in New York City, **$5-7.**

Postcard picturing bandleader
Sammy Kaye, **$1-2.**

Postcard of Smiling Jack Smith,
personally autographed, **$2-3.**

Postcard of Constance Talmadge,
$4-5. Movie star postcards are
becoming highly collectible.

Postcard of Janet Gaynor, **$5-6.**

JACKIE COOGAN

AMERICAN MOVIE STARS

NAME...

GRADE..

A notepad (lined paper was never used) with Jackie Coogan on the cover. For those too young to remember Jackie Coogan as a child star, try Uncle Fester on the television series "The Adams Family"! **$20-25.**

Gisele MacKenzie

Postcard of Gisele MacKenzie, one of the stars from "Your Hit Parade." This author remembers her playing a duet from time to time with Jack Benny. $1-2.

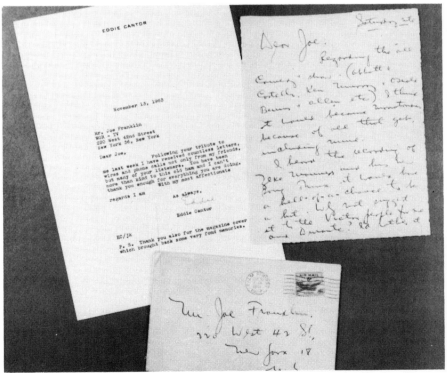

Two of the many personal letters from Eddie Cantor to Joe Franklin. Joe has an extensive collection of letters and autographs. He warns collectors to buy from reputable sources to avoid forgeries. Authentic autographs are valuable, and letters in personality's own hand are even more so.

Films

All the films listed are from Joe Franklin's collection. Joe's library consists of all varieties of films, encompassing countless subjects and stars. All films are 16mm black/white unless otherwise noted. Values may vary in different parts of the country.

A Night at the Opera, the Marx Brothers, **$250-300.**
A Star Is Born, Judy Garland, James Mason, **$600-700.**
Alamo, The, John Wayne, Kodachrome, scope, **$500-550.**
Angel Face, Robert Mitchum, **$275-300.**
Animal Crackers, the Marx Brothers, **$225-250.**
At War with the Army, Dean Martin and Jerry Lewis, **$200-250.**
Back in the Saddle, Gene Autry, **$150-175.**
Battle Cry, Aldo Ray, Tab Hunter, color, **$225-250.**
Bedtime for Bonzo, Ronald Reagan, **$150-175.**
Big Broadcast, 1938, Bob Hope, **$200-250.**
Black Cat, The, 1941, Basil Rathbone, Bela Lugosi, Alan Ladd, **$250-275.**
Black Gold, Phil Carey, **$80-90.**
Blonde Venus, Marlene Dietrich, **$350-400.**
Bohemian Girl, Laurel and Hardy, **$175-200.**
Branded, Buck Jones, **$150-175.**
Bus Stop, Marilyn Monroe, scope/color, **$250-300.**
Cocoanuts, the Marx Brothers, **$225-250.**
Come and Get It, Frances Farmer, **$275-300.**
Come Back Little Sheba, Shirley Booth, Burt Lancaster, color, **$300-400.**
Cornered, Tim McCoy, **$125-150.**
Countess From Hong Kong, Marlon Brando, Sophia Loren, color, **$225-275.**
Dangerous When Wet, Esther Williams, color, **$300-350.**
Dream Girl, Betty Hutton, **$100-125.**
Everybody Sing, Judy Garland, **$300-350.**
Flying Deuces, The, Laurel and Hardy, **$200-250.**
Gold Diggers of 1935, Dick Powell, **$300-350.**
Gold Rush, The, Charlie Chaplin, dupes generally are available at **$150-175.**
Gold Rush, The, condensed one-hour version with narration, **$175-200.**
He Who Gets Slapped, Lon Chaney, **$250-275.**
Hard Day's Night, the Beatles, **$250-300.**
Hunchback of Notre Dame, Lon Chaney, **$150-200.**
In a Lonely Place, Humphrey Bogart, Gloria Graham, **$275-325.**
It Ain't Hay, Abbott and Costello, **$200-225.**
It Came From Outer Space, 3D, **$275-325.**
King Kong, the original version, **$225-250.**
Lifeboat, Tallulah Bankhead, **$300-400.**
Little Caesar, Edward G. Robinson, **$250-275.**
Maltese Falcon, The, Humphrey Bogart, **$300-400.**
March of the Wooden Soldiers, Laurel and Hardy, **$150-175.**
Mississippi, W.C. Fields, **$225-250.**
My Pal the King, Tom Mix, Mickey Rooney, **$200-250.**

On the Waterfront, Marlon Brando, **$250-275.**
Operation Pacific, John Wayne, **$200-225.**
Phantom Ranger, Tim McCoy, **$150-175.**
Psycho, Anthony Perkins, Janet Leigh, **$275-300.**
Punch Drunks, the Three Stooges, **$85-100.**
Rebel Without a Cause, James Dean, Natalie Wood, Sal Mineo, color, **$300-350.**
Red Snow, The, Guy Madison, **$80-90.**
Ride, Tenderfoot Ride, Gene Autry, **$175-200.**
Road to Rio, Bob Hope, Bing Crosby, Dorothy Lamour, **$225-250.**
Road to Utopia, Bing Crosby, Bob Hope, **$150-175.**
Roaring Ranger, Durango Kid, **$125-150.**
Silver Chalice, The, Paul Newman, **$125-150.**
Singin' in the Rain, Gene Kelly, Debbie Reynolds, color, **$275-350.**
Singing Cowboy, Gene Autry, **$175-200.**
Some Like It Hot, Marilyn Monroe, Jack Lemmon, Tony Curtis, **$350-400.**
Son of Kong, Robert Armstrong, **$165-175.**
Spurs, Hoot Gibson, **$200-250.**
Sting, The, Paul Newman, Robert Redford, **$200-225.**
Storm Warning, Ronald Reagan, **$200-225.**
Sunset Boulevard, Gloria Swanson, William Holden, **$250-275.**
Tarzan and the Amazons, Johnny Weissmuller, **$200-225.**
Tarzan and the Mermaids, Johnny Weissmuller, **$200-225.**
Thief of Baghdad, The, Douglas Fairbanks, Blackhawk silent with music added, **$400-500.**
Up in Arms, Danny Kaye, color, **$250-300.**
Woman Obsessed, Susan Hayward, color, **$75-100.**
Yankee Doodle Dandy, James Cagney, **$250-300.**
You Can't Cheat an Honest Man, W. C. Fields, Edgar Bergen, **$175-200.**

Shorts
A Doggone Story, Castle, **$10-20.**
Hi De Ho, Cab Calloway and his orchestra, **$35-50.**
King, The, and The Cowboy, 400', Tom Mix, Mickey Rooney, Castle, **$35-50.**
Little Lost Scent, Castle, **$20-30.**
Monogram Bloopers, **$25-35.**
Nairobi Trio, Ernie Kovac's Show, **$25-35.**
Rear Gunner, Ronald Reagan, 1942, 17 minutes, **$75-85.**
Smitherins, 1100', Laurel and Hardy, **$50-75.**
Space Ship Happy, the Three Stooges, **$80-100.**
Three Bruins Go Camping, **$20-25.**
Two Toes, silent, Laurel and Hardy, **$75-100.**
Western Honor, Kirby Grant, **$25-35.**

Cartoons
Betty Boop's Penthouse, Betty Boop, **$25-35.**
Buzz Saw Battler, 100', Donald Duck, silent, 1934, **$10-15.**

Koko's Earth Control, silent, **$25-35.**
Papa Yogi, Yogi Bear, **$15-20.**

Trailers
Captain Blood, **$20-25.**
Danger in the Pacific, Leo Carrillo, **$15-20.**
My Gal Loves Music, Bob Crosby, **$15-20.**
On Stage, Everybody, Jack Oakie, **$15-20.**
Psycho, 6 minutes, **$25-35.**

Television shows
Alfred Hitchcock, "Don't Bother To Knock," **$75-100.**
Checkmate, "The Human Touch," **$75-100.**
Death Valley Days, "Ten Feet of Nothing," **$30-40.**
Have Gun, Will Travel, "A Miracle for St. Francis," **$40-50.**
I Spy, "Crusade To Limbo," **$75-100.**
It Takes a Thief, "The Packager," **$100-125.**
Lucy Show, The, "Lucy Takes Up Golf," **$50-75.**
Millionaire, The, "Sally Sims," **$60-75.**
Outer Limits, "The Brain of Colonel Barham," **$100-125.**
Wild Wild West, The, "Cossacks," **$75-100.**

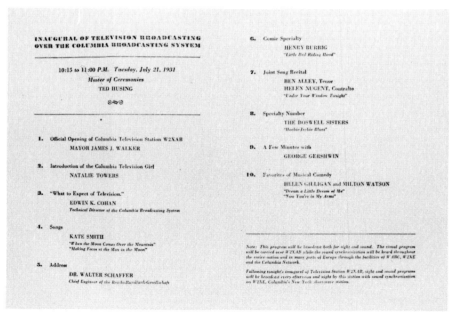

*The inaugural program, featuring Kate Smith singing "When the Moon Comes Over the Mountain" and "Making Faces at the Man in the Moon," a specialty number by George Gershwin; and the Boswell Sisters singing "Heebie-Jeebie Blues." **$200-250.***

192

Early television program for the All Star Revue, with Ezio Pinza, Jack Carson, Jimmy Durante, Olsen and Johnson, Danny Thomas, and Ed Wynn, September 8, 1951, $15-20.

Stills

All the movie stills and photographs in this section are from Joe's archives, and they all are highly collectible. Where possible, values have been listed. The values are for stills in mint condition. Keep in mind that prices vary and are dependent on the area of the country in which you live, the availability of the still, the condition, and provenance.

Anyone doing research in this area, whether it's for a book, project, article, or just for personal enlightenment, can pay up to $200 for the rental of a single still. It would seem a wiser approach to merely make personal acquisitions, which can lead to a collection of important historical material.

Ramon Navarro, $10-15.

Betty Furness, $1-5.

Robert Montgomery, **$10-12.**

The movie still for Ali Baba Goes to Town. *Joe prefers his stills without autographs.* **$7-10.**

Peter Lawford, autographed, **$10-12.**

Michael Redgrave, **$5-8.**

*Lyle Talbot,
autographed, 1940,
$10-15.*

Ann Harding, 1934, $10-12.

Rosalind Russell, $10-12.

EDWARD G. ROBINSON · IDA LUPINO · JOHN GARFIELD in "THE SEA WOLF"—A Warner Bros.—First National Picture

One of Joe's favorite movies, The Sea Wolf, *with Edward G. Robinson, 1947,* **$5-10.**

Freddie Bartholomew, Jackie Cooper, and Mickey Rooney in The Devil Is a Sissy, **$15-20.**

WARNER BROS. PICTURES Present EDWARD G. ROBINSON · IDA LUPINO · JOHN GARFIELD · BARRY FITZGERALD in "THE SEA WOLF"

Co-star in The Sea
Wolf, *Ida Lupino,
1947* **$5-10.**

SHIRLEY TEMPLE
"SUSANNAH OF THE MOUNTIES"   R58/165

*Shirley Temple, 1938
in a scene from*
Susannah of the
Mounties, **$30-40.**

197

Ernest Borgnine,
1967, **$1-5.**

A scene from
Scarface, *with Paul*
Muni (Scarface), Ka-
ren Morley (Poppy),
and George Raft
(Rinaldo), **$20-25.**

John Barrymore,
1927, **$10-15.**

Dana Andrews, **$5-8.**

199

A scene from Love Thy Neighbor, *star-ring Jack Benny and Fred Allen, 1940,* **$15-20.**

Bud Abbott and Lou Costello in a scene from The Noose Hangs High, *1948,* **$10-20.**

A scene from "THE NOOSE HANGS HIGH"
An Eagle-Lion Production

200

Robert Taylor, **$10-12.**

Nelson Eddy, **$10-15.**

Greta Garbo and Bela Lugosi in a scene from Ninotchka, **$40-50.**

Rock Hudson, **$5-8.**

Fred Astaire and Ginger Rogers in Follow the Fleet, **$10-15.**

Joe Penner in Paramount's feature College Rhythm, *1934,* **$15-20.** *(A bit of trivia: The name of Joe Penner's duck was Goo Goo.)*

Greer Garson, auto-graphed, **$10-12.**

Michael Rennie, **$5-8.**

"Joe Franklin is an excellent interviewer. He's good to his guests because he lets them do a great deal of the talking. I'm also grateful to Joe for the wonderful things he has said on behalf of St. Jude's Children's Research Center during the many times I have appeared on his show."

—Danny Thomas

"Joe Franklin is a warm and gentle man. He makes his guests feel special and loved. He does his homework and has total knowledge of his guests and their endeavors. He lets his guests speak their mind. In my opinion, he has become as much a legend as anyone he has ever interviewed. He makes his guests and audience feel happy. He is always up and consistent and I love him dearly."

—Vivian Blaine

About the Author

Sandra Andacht is the editor and publisher of *The Orientalia Journal.* Her column, "East Meets West/Exploring Orientalia" is a regular feature of *The Antique Trader Weekly.* Mrs. Andacht is the editor of "The Orientalia Journal Column" which appears in numerous publications on antiques throughout the country. She is also the editor and publisher of *The Orientalia Journal Annual of Articles.* Mrs. Andacht is the author of *Treasury of Satsuma; Satsuma: An Illustrated Guide; Wallace-Homestead Price Guide to Oriental Antiques* (first and second editions). Mrs. Andacht's numerous articles, covering all aspects of Orientalia, have appeared in publications such as *Andon, Arts of Asia Magazine, Antique Monthly, Interior Design Magazine,* and others.

Mrs. Andacht is a dealer, collector, lecturer, research consultant, and appraiser (a member of the New England Appraisers Assoc.) and is called upon in this capacity by the United States Customs Service among others. She is a faculty member of Yeshiva University's Appraisal Studies Program, and teaches Oriental Decorative Arts (Continuing Education Program) at the New York City downtown facility. Mrs. Andacht also participates in the various art and antiques seminars presented by Yeshiva University in addition to her program on Connoisseurship.

Sandra Andacht is a member of Netsuke Kenkyukai; The International Chinese Snuff Bottle Society; Vereniging voor Japanese Kunst (Society for Japanese Arts & Crafts); The Oriental Art Society of Chicago; and the Louis Comfort Tiffany Society (this in connection with Tiffany's collections of Orientalia and his accoutrements for Orientalia).

"Joe is a very warm individual and a well-informed interviewer. He has a good sense of humor, which is very important when you're chatting with a fellow. He is a landmark in New York City, and it's always nice to see him and hear from him. I fondly remember the times I appeared on his show."

—Bob Hope

"First, I'd like to thank Joe, on his thirty-five years, for being one of the best TV interviewers. Every time I have appeared with Joe, it's been a revelation because of his unique style of interviewing people and bringing the worst and best out of them. He has that magnetic knack of asking the right questions. Unfortunately, some of us have forgotten what a pioneer talk show host Joe was.

"I will continue to be Joe's biggest fan because I think he is one of the greatest. You can always select the very few who are in that category by their sustained success."

—Milton Berle

"Joe Franklin and I have strolled down memory lane for so many years that I suspect we may have forgotten when and where we first met. We have both watched radio thrive, almost die, and then thrive again after television's explosion on the American entertainment scene. But Joe's wonderful ability to evoke the past just rolls on and on, happily making the transition from radio to TV look easy. What's the secret? Joe's never failing good humor, the people of entertainment history, and the warmth to make his listeners and viewers comfortable as they travel down memory lane."

—John Gambling, of WOR Radio

"The Lady in the Harbor symbolizes freedom, the Public Library lions represent learning, and Joe Franklin means show business for generations of born and bred New Yorkers. Joe may be hailed as the 'unofficial Mayor of New York,' but I wonder if that title does him any justice. A lot of mayors have come and gone while Joe has looked down on Times Square.

"New Yorkers have no need of time capsules as long as we have a vital, voluble institution in his own time known as Joe Franklin."

—New York State Senator Frank Padavan